access to history

GOVERNMENT *and* REFORM: BRITAIN 1815–1918

Second Edition

Robert Pearce and Roger Stearn

& Stoughton

E HODDE HEADLINE GROUP

Acknowledgements

The front cover shows John Bright by W W Ouless, reproduced courtesy of the National Portrait Gallery, London.

The publishers would like to thank the following individuals, institutions and companies for permission to reproduce copyright illustrations in this book:
The British Museum, pages 19, 109; Cambridge University Library, pages 41, 112; Illustrated London News, pages 57, 60; Punch, pages 62, 139.

Every effort has been made to trace and acknowledge ownership of copyright. The publishers will be glad to make suitable arrangements with any copyright holders whom it has not been possible to contact.

Orders: please contact Bookpoint Ltd, 78 Milton Park, Abingdon, Oxon OX14 4TD. Telephone (44) 01235 827720, Fax: (44) 01235 400454. Lines are open from 9.00–6.00, Monday to Saturday, with a 24 hour message answering service. Email address: orders@bookpoint.co.uk

British Library Cataloguing in Publication Data
A catalogue record for this title is available from the British Library

ISBN 0 340 78947 6

First published 1994
Impression number 10 9 8 7 6 5 4 3 2 1
Year   2005 2004 2003 2002 2001 2000

Typeset by Fakenham Photosetting Limited, Fakenham, Norfolk
Printed in Great Britain for Hodder & Stoughton Educational, a division of Hodder Headline Plc, 338 Euston Road, London NW1 3BH by Redwood Books Ltd.

Contents

Preface

To the general reader

Although the *Access to History* series has been designed with the needs of students studying the subject at higher examination levels very much in mind, it also has a great deal to offer the general reader. The main body of the text (i.e. ignoring the 'Study Guides' at the ends of chapters) forms a readable and yet stimulating survey of a coherent topic as studied by historians. However, each author's aim has not merely been to provide a clear explanation of what happened in the past (to interest and inform): it has also been assumed that most readers wish to be stimulated into thinking further about the topic and to form opinions of their own about the significance of the events that are described and discussed (to be challenged). Thus, although no prior knowledge of the topic is expected on the reader's part, she or he is treated as an intelligent and thinking person throughout. The author tends to share ideas and possibilities with the reader, rather than passing on numbers of so-called 'historical truths'.

To the student reader

Although advantage has been taken of the publication of a second edition to ensure the results of recent research are reflected in the text, the main alteration from the first edition is the inclusion of new features, and the modification of existing ones, aimed at assisting you in your study of the topic at AS level, A level and Higher. Two features are designed to assist you during your first reading of a chapter. The *Points to Consider* section following each chapter title is intended to focus your attention on the main theme(s) of the chapter, and the issues box following most section headings alerts you to the question or questions to be dealt with in the section. The *Working on ...* section at the end of each chapter suggests ways of gaining maximum benefit from the chapter.

There are many ways in which the series can be used by students studying History at a higher level. It will, therefore, be worthwhile thinking about your own study strategy before you start your work on this book. Obviously, your strategy will vary depending on the aim you have in mind, and the time for study that is available to you.

If, for example, you want to acquire a general overview of the topic in the shortest possible time, the following approach will probably be the most effective:

1. Read chapter 1. As you do so, keep in mind the issues raised in the *Points to Consider* section.

2. Read the *Points to Consider* section at the beginning of chapter 2 and decide whether it is necessary for you to read this chapter.
3. If it is, read the chapter, stopping at each heading or sub-heading to note down the main points that have been made. Often, the best way of doing this is to answer the question(s) posed in the *Key Issues* boxes.
4. Repeat stage 2 (and stage 3 where appropriate) for all the other chapters.

If, however, your aim is to gain a thorough grasp of the topic, taking however much time is necessary to do so, you may benefit from carrying out the same procedure with each chapter, as follows:

1. Try to read the chapter in one sitting. As you do this, bear in mind any advice given in the *Points to Consider* section.
2. Study the flow diagram at the end of the chapter, ensuring that you understand the general 'shape' of what you have just read.
3. Read the *Working on …* section and decide what further work you need to do on the chapter. In particularly important sections of the book, this is likely to involve reading the chapter a second time and stopping at each heading and sub-heading to think about (and probably to write a summary of) what you have just read.
4. Attempt the *Source-based questions* section. It will sometimes be sufficient to think through your answers, but additional understanding will often be gained by forcing yourself to write them down.

When you have finished the main chapters of the book, study the 'Further Reading' section and decide what additional reading (if any) you will do on the topic.

This book has been designed to help make your studies both enjoyable and successful. If you can think of ways in which this could be done more effectively, please contact us. In the meantime, we hope that you will gain greatly from your study of History.

Keith Randell & Robert Pearce

1 Introduction: the Development of Democracy in Britain

POINTS TO CONSIDER

This chapter is designed to give you with an overview of electoral reform in Britain and so to provide you with the broad historical context for the chapters that follow. Hence you need to grasp the main issues and themes rather than to take detailed notes.

Around the middle of the nineteenth century an extensive debate took place in Britain on the nature, and desirability, of 'democracy'. Should the vote in general elections be limited, as in the past, to those who had special qualifications, including the ownership of property and thus an economic stake in the country? Those who said 'Yes' asserted two principles. They argued that historical precedent was important – since a system that had worked well in the past would surely continue to do so – and that the wealthy were naturally superior to the poor, whom they dismissed as their 'social inferiors' or even as the 'swinish multitude'. But others insisted that the dead hand of the past should be removed from government. Some of these people believed that education was the key to the responsible exercise of the franchise. In their view, the country should be governed by men of proven ability, since only the well-educated and intelligent would be able to grapple with the problems of the modern world. Perhaps those of special merit might qualify for extra votes, over and above those conferred on ordinary voters? Another group called for universal male suffrage (one man, one vote), believing that every man had the *right* to vote. In their view, all men had been created equal and therefore all were entitled to an equal say in the way they were governed. A small but growing number also maintained that women should have the vote on precisely the same terms as men.

Never before had there been such a thorough exchange of views on the electoral system; and the debate did not stop at the issue of who should vote. There was also the question of how. Should electors continue to declare their support for a candidate in public, or might a secret ballot, to shield electors from intimidation, be preferable? In addition, what qualifications should a candidate have? Might the existing system, whereby only the wealthy could stand for parliament, be beneficially reformed? Finally, should the system of constituencies be changed? Was it fair that some candidates were elected by tens of thousands of voters, while others, in much smaller constituencies, need poll only a few hundred votes?

The general consensus of opinion was that the existing arrangements could be improved, but most political philosophers fought shy of universal suffrage. It was generally thought that, while the franchise might well be extended, a truly mass electorate would lead to a debasement of politics. If everyone could vote there would be a 'tyranny of the masses'. To most Victorians, therefore, 'democracy' was almost a term of abuse: it meant election by the uneducated, incompetent many. The system we know today, where virtually everyone can vote, came to be accepted only slowly and with great reluctance.

Similar debates had been going on, sporadically, ever since a form of democracy had been instituted in Athens in the fifth century BC. The word 'democracy' means rule by the '*demos*', translated as either the 'people' (by those who approve of the system) or the 'mob' (by those who do not). In Athens, a small city-state, all free men had been able to take part directly in governing themselves, and this system had provided inspiration for later generations. But the Athenian example could not be directly copied. Such a 'direct democracy' (in which all citizens participated in person) could not possibly work in much larger communities: instead, nineteenth-century democrats judged that an 'indirect' or 'representative' democracy would be more suitable. This is a system in which government is carried on by elected representatives of the people. But who should elect these representatives? Even in Athens not everyone participated in politics, since slaves and women were excluded; and the majority of Victorians insisted that, whereas representatives should be elected to look after the interests of all, they should be chosen by only limited numbers of the people. It can thus be seen that the Victorian debate was carried on within agreed parameters. Everyone – or almost everyone – agreed with the idea of representative government: the controversy centred on how representative, and therefore democratic, it should be.

1 Historical Survey

> **KEY ISSUE** How did British government evolve before 1800?

For much of British history, democracy was not even debated. After the Norman conquest of 1066 the government of England was a feudal monarchy. The monarch ruled with the assistance of (or sometimes in conflict with) the aristocracy, the leading landowners of the realm. In some towns the citizens acquired limited rights of self-government, but the majority of the population had no share in local or national government. The monarch's rule depended, ultimately, on the strength of his armed forces, as well as on his own physical prowess. Hence most monarchs were themselves warriors. Government therefore rested on force, rather than on the organised consent that characterises democracy. Kings who sought some theoretical justification for their rule turned to the church: monarchs, it was said, ruled by 'divine right', deriving their powers from God.

In the thirteenth century a parliament (an assembly with representatives from all over the kingdom) was set up and slowly developed. It contained members of the land-owning nobility and leading figures from the church in the 'upper' house, while in the 'lower' house representatives of the shires and some of the towns were elected by a small minority of the population. Here lay the origins of the later politically powerful House of Commons, but such was certainly not the intention of those who first set up this body. Parliament was there, initially, to help the monarch to govern effectively – to help him collect taxation and to secure acceptance for his laws. The king's business dominated its proceedings.

Important developments occurred in the Tudor period (1485–1603), when parliament became an accepted institution of the state. The House of Commons even began to make criticisms of royal policy, and its relations with the Crown were not always good. They deteriorated much more under the early Stuart kings, and in particular there was friction with Charles I, whose belief in the divine right of kings was coming to be challenged by some of his subjects. He governed without calling a parliament for 11 years, from 1629 to 1640. When the need for money forced him to recall parliament, conflict with the majority in the Commons over a wide range of issues escalated into civil war. Charles lost and was executed in 1649. Britain then became a republic, and important political debates took place which in some ways anticipated those of Victorian England. A democratic group, the Levellers, asserted the natural right of men to vote, and apparently wanted universal manhood suffrage. They also argued that the representation given to a particular area of the country should be proportionate to its population. However, their opponents, led by Oliver Cromwell, claimed that only those with substantial property should vote. The Levellers were crushed (though their views did later influence radicals in Victorian England). England without a king did not become a democracy; instead Cromwell ruled as Lord Protector. Yet, although he rejected the democratic views of the Levellers, he nevertheless restructured the old electoral system, disfranchising many of the smaller towns and providing seats in parliament for some of the larger ones, such as Leeds and Manchester.

The death of Cromwell was followed by the restoration in 1660 of the monarchy in the person of Charles II. The upheavals of the civil war and the republic had alarmed the ruling classes and increased their conservatism. Henceforth they distrusted change and wanted stability. Cromwell's electoral reforms were reversed. Indeed for the next hundred years there was no real demand for parliamentary reform: within the ruling elites the desire to make the House of Commons more representative of the people simply did not exist. England's government was certainly monarchical: ministers, for instance, were chosen personally by the king, and only he could dismiss them. But this is not to say that England resumed in 1660 where it had left off before the civil war. Monarchs had learned that they were mortal and that power had to be shared with parliament, which was a permanent and important institution. Certainly no king, henceforth, tried to rule without it.

In the 1680s James II, Charles II's successor, did try to increase the powers of the monarchy but he was deposed. The republican experiment, however, was not tried a second time. Instead, William of Orange, a Dutchman with a claim to the throne by marriage, became king. Monarchical government was preserved, and when the last of the Stuarts died without heir, a Hanoverian became monarch as George I and began a new dynasty. The essential powers of the monarch were preserved: he was Head of State and he chose and dismissed ministers. But royal ministers were now invariably leading figures from parliament: indeed only if they had this position could they hope to secure that parliamentary approval for their policies which was a precondition for effective government. Government was thus a partnership between monarch and parliament; but as the eighteenth century wore on it became clear that it was parliament whose powers were in the ascendant.

Of course Britain was still not a democracy, because parliament was neither democratically elected nor representative of the people. In many ways Britain, around 1800, was an aristocracy, in that it was ruled by landowners and aristocrats. (Literally, 'aristocracy' means 'rule by the best', and the landowners certainly thought of themselves in this way, though they were to be described by the radical William Cobbett as 'a prodigious band of spongers, living upon the labour of the industrious part of the community'.) Blenheim Palace, Woburn Abbey, Hatfield House, Chatsworth and other magnificent stately homes are today familiar tourist attractions; but in the eighteenth and nineteenth centuries they were symbols of status and wealth and centres of aristocratic power. The aristocrats not only owned much of Britain, they also controlled its government. Parliament was divided between the Whigs, a party of rich aristocrats, and the Tories, another party of rich aristocrats. They dominated the House of Lords as a matter of course, since their birth gave them seats as of right, and they also dominated the House of Commons through an electoral system which was weighted in favour of the rich. Neither group, therefore, had any interest in electoral reform, realising that any changes might harm their easy dominance.

2 Growth of Democracy

> **KEY ISSUE** In what ways did the electoral system become more democratic after 1832?

Nevertheless reform did come. As we shall see in the following chapters, the distribution of political power changed slowly but nevertheless significantly. As the nineteenth century proceeded the monarch and the aristocracy lost power, and the middle classes – and to some extent the working classes – gained it. The system retained its traditional institutions (the monarchy, the House of Lords and the House of Commons, as well as parliamentary elections) but it became more representative and more democratic. The first important change came in 1832 with the Great Reform Act, so-called not so much because of the large number of people to whom it gave the vote but because it established the precedents of extending the vote to previously unenfranchised groups and of breaking tradition by redistributing seats. There were further reform acts in 1867, 1884–5 and 1918. Perhaps equally important, a secret ballot was introduced in 1872, together with effective legislation against corruption in 1883.

The electoral system became more democratic through a combination of factors: (i) an extension of the franchise which increased the electorate, (ii) changes in the distribution of seats to correspond more closely to the distribution of population, (iii) the removal of limitations on who could stand as candidates, and (iv) legislation against corruption and in favour of secret voting. Local government, an area which most Victorians considered even more important than national politics, was also made more democratic.

It was in the sphere of local government that women were first allowed to participate in British political life. At the start of the nineteenth century, women were excluded from the political system, except that a woman might become the monarch. The limited progress made towards female suffrage in the nineteenth century underlines how incomplete electoral reform was in the Britain of Queen Victoria. Only in 1918 were some women given the vote, and only in 1928 did women receive the vote on the same terms as men. Clearly, no system can be called democratic which excludes half the population.

3 Causation and Historical Debate

> **KEY ISSUE** Why was the political system reformed?

To some degree, electoral reform was a reflection of social and economic changes. Between the eighteenth and the twentieth centuries there was a transformation of Britain: the population increased, the number and size of towns grew and industrialisation proceeded apace. Industry replaced agriculture as the dominant sector of the economy, producing new wealthy groups who wanted a share of political power. There were also substantial improvements in science, technology, transport and communications. Such changes almost demanded a parallel modernisation of politics and government.

In addition to general factors, each reform was the result of a unique combination of specific factors. One might say that change came about because there was demand both outside and within parliament: a substantial section of the public desired reform, while politicians introduced particular measures which they believed would prove acceptable to the public and which, in some way, would benefit their own party. The relative importance of the different factors, and of particular individuals, varied from measure to measure.

a) Whig Interpretations

In the nineteenth century many Britons were very proud of their constitution and of the way in which it was evolving. The radical politician John Bright, for instance, declared that 'England is the mother of parliaments': he believed that the political structures being evolved at home were sure to be copied by other countries abroad. Historians of the time developed what has been called the 'Whig interpretation of history'. At the root of this was national pride: Britain was the most successful country in the world and would be used as a model by other nations which had the misfortune not to be British. In particular, they believed that British politics had evolved in an exemplary way: from a powerful medieval monarchy to a parliamentary regime. The monarch still existed but was largely a figurehead: power now rested with representatives elected by an electorate whose numbers could be increased as more people became able to exercise the franchise responsibly. The key breakthrough had come in 1832 with the Reform Act: a system that had been corrupt and unrepresentative had been wisely – and peacefully – replaced. Whereas other nations suffered upheaval and even bloody revolution, Britain had a system that allowed peaceful change. In the words of the historian Thomas Babington Macaulay, the key to Britain's success was the advice 'Reform, that you may preserve'; as a result, the British constitution was well-nigh perfect, and the country's history was 'emphatically the history of progress'.

Clearly, the Whig historians did not study the past for its own sake: they studied history with at least one eye firmly focused on the present, and to them the past was significant because it led on to the greatness of the present day. According to this school of thought, the electoral reforms of the nineteenth century were all part of one continuous process. One reform led on necessarily to another, so that the whole sequence of changes was virtually inevitable, and each of them was always for the best.

b) Modern Views

In the twentieth century most historians criticised the Whig interpretation as arrogant and naive. It is not so easy any more to see British history as a splendid process culminating in the glories of the present. After all, this country has declined as a Great Power and is no longer among the foremost economic powers, something that Macaulay and other nineteenth-century historians never predicted in their wildest nightmares. Nor have other countries flocked to copy our 'ideal' political forms (and those former colonies whose politics were modelled on Britain's at independence generally regretted adopting a system so alien to their own traditions). It is now generally believed that the 'Whigs' (who were often lawyers as well as historians) were far too concerned with legal and constitutional theories and that present-day historians should also investigate the realities of how political institutions functioned in practice and affected the lives of ordinary people. Whereas historians of the nineteenth century tended to be positive and optimistic, recent historians have on the whole been much more pessimistic and perhaps cynical, doubting whether any grandiose theory of history can ever explain the diversity of the human past and sometimes arguing that the truth about the past can never be recovered.

Nowadays historians try to examine the past without preconception by piecing together all the available evidence. This is often a time-consuming, indeed exhausting, business. As a result, most modern historians are specialists, concerned, for instance, not with the whole process of electoral reform but with specific reforms, or even with the effects of one act on a small number of constituencies. Owing to their efforts we now know far more than any Whig historian about the electoral reforms enacted after 1832. The following chapters summarise these recent findings. As a result, we can see definite weaknesses in the Whig interpretations. For instance, the pre-1832 system does not seem quite so uniformly corrupt as was once asserted, and nor does the succession of reform acts from 1832 onwards seem quite so enlightened. Often reforms resulted from the self-interested manoeuvres of politicians at Westminster rather than from sincerely-held principles. The growth of democracy is therefore hard to interpret as an inevitable process. Nor can the system that was evolved be seen, in any sense, as ideal or final.

It has been said that 'ignorance is the first requisite of the historian – ignorance, which simplifies and clarifies, which selects and omits'. Certainly it must have been much easier to write history in the nineteenth century than it is today. Our extensive knowledge makes it very difficult to generalise about the process of electoral reform from 1832 onwards. Indeed present-day historians disagree about the precise causes and effects of every major reform, and no doubt future research will fragment the already complicated picture still further. But at least we are able to see that the old, Whig generalisations were at best half-true and at worst positively misleading. Our uncertainties are founded on the bedrock of fact, whereas the old certainties resulted from the quicksand of fancy.

Working on Chapter 1

It is important to grasp i) the general evolution of the British political system before the nineteenth century, ii) the meaning of the term 'democracy' and why most Victorians were suspicious of it, and iii) the meaning of the 'Whig interpretation of history'.

Summary Diagram
The Development of Democracy in Britain

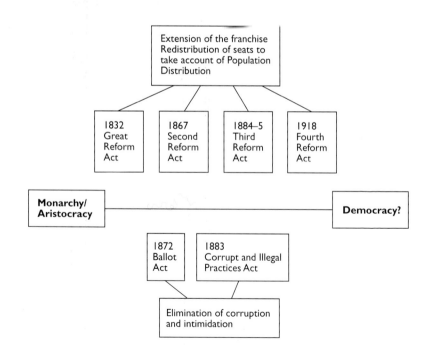

2 The Unreformed Political System

POINTS TO CONSIDER

This chapter introduces you to the political system before the Reform Act of 1832. You need to understand not only the main features of the system but also the criticisms and defences of it which were made by people at the time. Most important of all, you have to decide why it became impossible to maintain it during the era of socio-economic change in the nineteenth century.

KEY DATES

1789 Start of the French Revolution, boosting demands for reform in Britain.

1790 Publication of Burke's *Reflections on the Revolution in France* (anti-revolution).

1791 Publication of Paine's *Rights of Man* (pro-reform).

1800 Act of Union with Ireland: end of Irish Parliament, Irish MPs and Peers now at Westminster.

1807 Yorkshire election cost a record £250,000.

1820 Publication of Wade's *Black Book* (pro-reform).

At the end of the eighteenth century Britain was governed, as it is now, by the monarch, the House of Lords and the House of Commons. Yet the monarchy was far more powerful then, and the House of Lords also wielded much more power and influence. Indeed eighteenth-century government has been described, alternatively, as essentially monarchical or essentially aristocratic. Yet the most glaring contrast between politics around 1800 and today lies with the third element of the trinity, the House of Commons. Superficially, there are similarities: men sat at Westminster representing their constituents and using many of the same parliamentary procedures that have been preserved to the present day. But there was in fact little semblance of 'democracy' about this system: not only were all women and the vast majority of men ineligible to vote, but electoral contests were the exception rather than the rule. The House of Commons around 1800 was indeed remarkably unrepresentative of the British people, and many contemporaries condemned the whole political system as scandalously undemocratic and corrupt.

To modern eyes the electoral machinery of the pre-1832 period seems remarkably ill-fitted to produce a representative House of Commons. This is not surprising: it was not designed to do so. Parliament had originally been instituted by monarchs to obtain the acceptance to taxation of powerful magnates, who formed the House of Lords, and knights of the shires and other important individuals, who came together as the Commons. The machinery was devised to tap the wealth of the country not provide ideal democratic represen-tation. Important 'interests' were represented; but there was no attempt to make parliament representative of the people as a whole.

1 Pre-1832 Electoral Machinery

> **KEY ISSUE** What were the main characteristics of the unreformed electoral system?

a) Constituencies

The House of Commons, after the 1800 Act of Union with Ireland, consisted of 658 MPs, two each for most of the counties and parlia-mentary boroughs in the United Kingdom (together with two each for the universities of Oxford and Cambridge, elected by their gradu-ates). The geographical distribution of seats had been established in previous centuries, so that by the start of the nineteenth century there was little correlation between the distribution of seats and of population. This stemmed partly from the fact that, under Tudor monarchs, a number of small, and therefore easily-controlled, con-stituencies had been created in order to place royal supporters in the Commons; but it was also a reflection of population growth and move-ment since earlier times. As a result, serious anomalies had been cre-ated. More than 20 boroughs which had once been thriving communities had declined significantly, in some cases to the point of disappearance, degenerating into what were called 'rotten boroughs'. One of the most notorious of these was Old Sarum (north of Salisbury), a hill where not a single person lived. It returned two MPs, who were chosen by its owner! On the other hand, many towns that were growing in importance – such as Manchester (with 182,000 inhabitants in 1831), Birmingham (with 144,000) and Leeds (with 123,000) – were not parliamentary boroughs and so had no rep-resentation of their own. At the start of the nineteenth century, 21 of the 49 largest English towns were not parliamentary boroughs.

There were also regional imbalances in the distribution of seats. English MPs were dominant but, due to the distribution of borough seats, some parts of England were grossly over-represented and others were greatly under-represented. In general terms, London and the north had too few MPs, whilst the south and west had too many, especially Cornwall with its total of 44 seats. Compared to the bor-oughs, the counties were greatly under-represented; and since all counties returned two MPs each, large counties were under-represented relative to smaller ones. Also Scotland, with 45 MPs, only one more than Cornwall, had insufficient representation compared with the rest of the United Kingdom.

b) The Franchise

Like everything else in the unreformed political system, the ability to vote in parliamentary elections was determined largely by a number of different long-established local traditions. It was not a right accorded to individuals based on a coherent nationwide system.

i) Counties

The nearest to a standard franchise was to be found in the English counties. This was the '40-shilling freeholder' qualification established by an act of 1430, by which the franchise was granted to those who held a 'freehold' whose rental value was at least 40 shillings per annum. This originally meant land, but over time it was generally extended to include offices in church or state or a guaranteed cash income of this amount. Yet it was not always clear whether a particular source of income did or did not qualify as a freehold. For example, in the 1803 Middlesex election the brewer, butler, bell-ringer and organ-blower of Westminster Abbey all voted in respect of their offices, but their votes were subsequently disallowed after a Commons investigation. The inhabitants of Scottish counties were treated much less generously. Only those who owned property valued around £100 could vote, a figure which excluded the great mass of the population.

ii) Boroughs

There was no standard borough franchise. Traditionally English parliamentary boroughs have been categorised into six main types.

Freemen boroughs, which generally contained the largest number of voters, comprised one-third of the English total, while the other types accounted for the remainder. The complexity of the system was compounded by the fact that some boroughs used several types of qualifications. Similarly, individuals might qualify for votes in more than one constituency. Indeed there was no limit to the number of 'plural votes' which individuals might exercise.

Types of English Boroughs

1   *Freemen.* All those with the status of 'freemen' were allowed to vote. Generally this status could be inherited from one's father, acquired by serving an apprenticeship in the borough, or received as an honour from the borough's corporation, but practices differed from place to place.
2   *Scot and lot.* All those who paid poor rates could vote.
3   *Burgage.* Owners of property with this ancient form of tenure, which

was often limited to the plots of land that had formed the borough when it was originally laid out, could vote.
4 *Corporation.* Only members of the local town council could vote. But as these councils were self-perpetuating (rather than elected), there was no element of democracy in this franchise.
5 *Potwalloper.* Resident householders ('who had a family and boiled a pot') could vote.
6 *Freeholder.* This was a similar franchise requirement to that of the counties.

c) The Electorate

No one knows how many people could vote, or actually did vote, in elections before 1832. Still less can we be certain what positions in society the electors occupied. The surviving sources are fragmentary and do not allow historians to do other than 'guesstimate' on these crucial questions.

There were no registers of electors, and so the returning officer for each constituency had to note down the names of those eligible to vote who actually turned up at the hustings to do so. Since there was no secret ballot, he also noted down the names of the candidates for whom they voted. This information was recorded in 'poll books', which are consequently a crucial source for the electoral historian. From poll books we know who voted and for whom; and by using them alongside tax records and other local information, we can often get a reasonable idea of the occupations and status of the voters, their religious affiliation and so on. Thousands of poll books survive, yielding a mass of data which can be most conveniently analysed with the aid of a computer; but even so, many poll books have perished. None are known to exist for Cornwall, for example. Nor should we assume that those which do survive are necessarily representative of the country as a whole. And, of course, poll books tell us nothing about those many constituencies where elections were uncontested.

i) Counties

The county electorate was larger and generally more representative than that in the boroughs. Since county constituencies were mostly rural, their electors included the gentry and middling orders of pre-industrial society (farmers, clergymen, lawyers, tradesmen and businessmen). There were also some self-employed skilled workers, including blacksmiths and cabinet-makers. The uniform 40-shilling freehold, however, did not produce a uniform electorate, since the value of land and property varied from one part of the country to the next. In some, though not all, constituencies, tenants as well as the owners of property voted.

In some areas urbanisation changed the county electorate. As towns which were not parliamentary boroughs grew, and as some cities and towns which were parliamentary boroughs grew beyond their legal borough boundaries, so the numbers and proportion of urban voters in county constituencies increased. London sprawled beyond its formal boundaries into the neighbouring counties, especially Middlesex; and the growth of Birmingham, Manchester and Leeds led to greater numbers of urban voters in the counties of Warwickshire, Lancashire and Yorkshire respectively. In such areas the electorate began to include the rising 'new men' of the 'industrial revolution' – factory owners, engineers and merchants.

County electorates varied greatly in size, but were usually thousands strong. At the extremes, Rutland had under 1,300 voters and Yorkshire over 16,000 (even though each county returned two MPs). However, with agricultural labourers unable to qualify for the vote, the proportion of adult males enfranchised in the counties was rarely more than 10 per cent, lower than in many boroughs.

ii) Boroughs

Borough electorates, with their numerous different qualifications for the franchise, were more varied than those in the counties. In 'rotten boroughs' the voters were simply employees or other nominees of the 'patron' (a polite term for the virtual owner of the constituency). In the corporation boroughs, the corporations (local councils) were small, exclusive groups, usually Anglican and Tory, of minor gentry, local businessmen and members of the professions. In some places they were independent, substantial citizens, in others the creatures of a local landowner. For example, at Marlborough the corporation consisted entirely of the steward, butler, footmen and other dependants of the Marquess of Aylesbury! Over half the English boroughs had electorates under 300, and over 50 boroughs had fewer than 50 voters each. Gatton in Surrey had seven.

In boroughs other than burgage and corporation boroughs, however, the franchise was sometimes held by a wide range of men including the poor, though those in receipt of poor relief were often disqualified. 43 English boroughs had over 1,000 voters, including 7 with over 5,000. The largest electorate was the scot and lot city of Westminster, which was estimated to total between 16,000 and 17,000 men. There was near universal male suffrage in such potwalloper boroughs as Cirencester and Honiton.

Recent research has shown that, overall, the borough electorate was socially and economically extensive. It was dominated by retailers and craftsmen of the middling orders. Probably about 40 per cent were craftsmen, 20 per cent retailers, 6 per cent merchants and manufacturers, 14 per cent gentlemen and professionals, and 14 per cent semi-skilled and unskilled workers. This was largely a pre-industrial electorate, dominated by small, independent producers and shopkeepers. It included both masters and employees. In some boroughs one occupational group was especially important: worsted weavers, for example, made up about a third of the Norwich electorate.

iii) Overall

One expert has compared the unreformed electorate to a blunted diamond in shape. At the top were gentlemen and professionals, then came a greater number of retailers and even more craftsmen, and finally there were a smaller number from unskilled and labouring occupations. The electorate was less narrow and more representative than was once assumed. Nevertheless it was far from democratic, excluding all women and the majority of men (including many middle-class and most working-class men). For the country as a whole, the counties probably contained about 55 per cent of the total electorate, although they had only 16 per cent of the seats, and on average individual county electorates were larger than those of boroughs.

It should be remembered, however, that the unreformed system was neither static nor inflexible. In its latter years the number of voters was growing rapidly – probably by more than 50 per cent between 1782 and 1832 – though not as fast as population growth. Historians have differed in their estimates of the total electorate. Exact numbers cannot be known, because of inadequate records and plural voting, but perhaps 11–16 per cent of adult males were eligible to vote at the start of the nineteenth century.

2 Elections

> **KEY ISSUE** How important were elections before 1832 and how were they conducted?

a) Uncontested

The size of the electorate is a good indication of the degree of democracy in the unreformed system. But it is not a foolproof one, since many elections were in fact uncontested. At the most, one-third of constituencies held contested elections in the century before 1832, and at some general elections the figure was much lower than this. In 1761 only 4 English counties (out of 40) and 42 boroughs (out of 202) held elections. County seats were often dominated by peers or local landowners, so making an election pointless because the result would have been a foregone conclusion; and sometimes rival families would agree to accept a seat each in a two-member constituency, thereby avoiding the expenses of holding a contest. Boroughs too were often entirely at the disposal of important individuals, especially those rotten boroughs with tiny electorates. Old Sarum was contested for the last time in 1715. Gatton was a typical 'proprietorial' (or 'pocket') borough, to be bought by the highest bidder, who would then avoid the need to stand for election against rivals. The auctioneer selling Gatton insisted that the purchaser would have

1 no tormenting claims of insolent electors to evade, no tinkers' wives to kiss, no impossible promises to make, none of the toilsome and not very clean paths of canvassing to drudge through; but, with his mind at ease and his conscience clear, with this elegant contingency in his
5 pocket, the honours of the state will await his plucking and with its emoluments his purse will overflow.

It was bought for £90,000 in 1801. Probably around half of Britain's MPs owed their seats to the patronage of wealthy individuals or the Crown. A majority in the Commons might therefore be formed by MPs who had in fact received no more than a few thousand votes between them.

b) Contested

The elections that were held varied so much that it is hard to generalise about them, though the traditional depiction has stressed their cynically corrupt nature. Elections had to be held at least once every seven years, though in practice they tended to be held more often. They were often dramatic and colourful affairs fought on a variety of national and local issues, with local affairs – and local rivalries between landowning families – much more to the fore than today. They were also expensive for the candidates and their backers. The Yorkshire election of 1807 cost a record, and ruinous, £250,000. It was customary, in counties and boroughs, for candidates to pay, when necessary, for their supporters' travel and accommodation (often expensive since even large counties had only a single polling station), as well as for generous 'treating' in the form of food and drink, especially drink. Borough elections in particular were often loud and rowdy affairs, marked by an unusual amount of drunkenness. There was also much 'colourable employment' (i.e. the temporary employment of men as 'messengers' and 'watchmen' to gain support).

Because voting was open and public, rather than by secret ballot, non-electors were encouraged to participate in the proceedings to influence the voters. They often took part in noisy processions, carrying banners daubed with appropriate slogans, all amidst a carnival atmosphere. It was good spectator sport, in which the spectators sometimes joined in. Less legitimately, there was often violence and intimidation. Some election agents hired gangs of criminals (known ironically as 'lambs') armed with clubs, to attack their opponents' supporters. Sometimes there was kidnapping of voters until the election was over (known as 'cooping') or, more subtly, the impersonation of dead or absent voters. Occasionally there were major riots and serious injuries.

The formal election proceedings opened with the public ceremony of the nomination of the candidates, which a journalist once described as follows:

1   The candidates were proposed and seconded in face of each other on a public platform ... in the presence of a vast tumultuous crowd, three-quarters of whom were generally drunk, and all of whom were inflamed by the passion of furious partisanship. Fortunate indeed was the orator
5   whose speech was anything more than a dumb show. Brass bands and drums not unusually accompanied the efforts of the speakers to make themselves heard. Brickbats, dead cats and rotten eggs came flying like bewildering meteors across the eyes of the rival politicians on the hustings. The crowds generally enlivened the time by a series of faction
10 fights among themselves.

The most famous account of a borough election is Charles Dickens's, in *The Pickwick Papers* (written after but set before the 1832 Reform Act), of the 'Eatanswill' election:

1   Then Horatio Fizkin, Esquire, of Fizkin Lodge, near Eatanswill, presented himself for the purpose of addressing the electors; which he no sooner did, than the band employed by the honourable Samuel Slumkey, commenced performing with a power to which their strength
5   in the morning was a trifle; in return for which, the Buff crowd belaboured the heads and shoulders of the Blue crowd; on which the Blue crowd endeavoured to dispossess themselves of their very unpleasant neighbours the Buff crowd; and a scene of struggling, and pushing, and fighting succeeded ...
10   The speeches of the two candidates, though differing in every other respect, afforded a beautiful tribute to the merit and high worth of the electors of Eatanswill. Both expressed their opinion that a more independent, a more enlightened, a more public-spirited, a more noble-minded, a more disinterested set of men than those who had promised
15 to vote for him, never existed on earth; each darkly hinted his suspicions that the electors in the opposite interest had certain swinish and besotted infirmities which rendered them unfit for the exercise of the important duties they were called upon to discharge ...
        During the whole time of the polling, the town was in a perpetual
20 fever of excitement ... Exciseable articles [alcoholic drinks] were remarkably cheap at the public-houses; and spring vans paraded the streets for the accommodation of voters who were seized with any temporary dizziness of the head ... A small body of electors remained unpolled on the very last day. They were calculating and reflective per-
25 sons, who had not yet been convinced by the arguments of either party, although they had had frequent conferences with each. One hour before the close of the poll, Mr Perker solicited the honour of a private interview with these intelligent, these noble, these patriotic men. It was granted. His arguments were brief, but satisfactory. They went in a
30 body to the poll ...

Many historians have concluded that Dickens's fictional account was not exaggerated. Yet we should beware of tarring all elections with such an exuberant, Dickensian brush. 'Eatanswill' may well have had its real-life equivalents, but not all contests followed this model. While 'treating' was usual, and indeed was considered normal and necessary, large-scale bribery and major violence were probably exceptional. An expert has classified only 20 boroughs as positively 'venal', with politics reduced solely to financial transactions. There was almost certainly an equal, and perhaps larger, number of 'open' constituencies, both county and borough, which saw vigorous, participatory electoral processes in which electors had choices and made them with political awareness. The great majority probably lay somewhere in the middle, being influenced but rarely totally dominated by patrons. Certainly in the country as a whole, politicians could not afford to ignore the electorate.

3 MPs and Political Power

> **KEY ISSUE** To what extent did members of the aristocracy dominate politics?

'Representatives' in the House of Commons were by no means representative of the British population. Catholics, Quakers and practising Jews could not become MPs, and neither could men who were not comparatively rich. Only those with property worth at least £600 a year could stand for a county constituency, while for boroughs the minimum was £300. To be elected they would have to pay for election expenses and for 'treating' voters and other members of the public; and once elected they would receive no salary. It was possible for a man of modest means to become an MP but usually only as the protégé of a rich man – more often than not, of a peer.

The situation fluctuated from one general election to another, but during the first 30 years of the nineteenth century about 200 seats in the House of Commons were controlled by peers. In 1826, for example, no fewer than 165 MPs were themselves members of the aristocracy, mostly the sons of peers. The aristocracy thus dominated the unreformed political system of Great Britain. They controlled a number of rotten boroughs, while elsewhere they triumphed through the deference of their tenants and other dependants and through judiciously high election expenditure. They owned so much land, had such wealth and status, controlled so many persons and so many local communities, that peers dominated politics. They held the key positions of power. Aristocrats were a majority in the cabinet; they *were* the House of Lords; and they dominated the House of Commons.

Yet the House of Commons also contained many members of the

upper-middle classes – bankers, merchants, industrialists and lawyers – and the occasional relatively impecunious middle-class radical. As a result, unreformed politics was not a 'closed' or exclusively aristocratic system: peers were prepared to share power with the gentry and the middle classes.

The political career was always open to exceptionally talented middle-class men, providing they secured a seat in parliament and were prepared to work the system. As for the majority of men, the system had not much to offer, only free drinks every few years.

4 Contemporary Criticisms of the System

> **KEY ISSUE** What aspects of the system did critics condemn, and what reforms did the want to see?

Radicals and others criticised the unreformed representative system through various media, including speeches, the press, books and cartoons (see 'The System' on page 19).

The most effective radical writer was Tom Paine, a man greatly influenced by the philosophers of the Enlightenment who insisted that governments should rest on the consent of the people. In 1791 he published the *Rights of Man*. Republican, iconoclastic and vivid, it condemned the existing society and constitution as the fraudulent and unjust exploitation of the majority for the benefit of the royal and aristocratic few. Paine demanded universal male suffrage: he wanted to see a government based not on the traditions of the past but on the natural rights of man and the sovereignty of the people. He condemned the existing system, with its narrow, illogical franchises, its rotten boroughs and corruption, as well as the unwarranted political power of the aristocracy and the monarchy (which he dismissed as 'a silly, contemptible thing'). Instead he demanded parliamentary reform and democracy. In his view, only a government elected by the people would have legitimacy.

The *Rights of Man* became a bestseller and was very influential. The following is an example of its arguments:

1 Can anything be more limited, and at the same time more capricious, than the qualifications of electors are in England? Limited – because not one man in a hundred ... is admitted to vote. Capricious – because the lowest character that can be supposed to exist, and who has not so
5 much as the visible means of an honest livelihood, is an elector in some places: while in other places, the man who pays very large taxes, and has a known fair character, and the farmer who rents to the amount of three or four hundred pounds a year, with a property on that farm to three or four times that amount, is not admitted to be an elector ...
10 The county of Yorkshire, which contains nearly a million of souls,

This cartoon, by the leading cartoonist George Cruikshank, was published in 1831. The House of Commons (St Stephen's) is shown as a water mill supported by cannons; the slats of the water wheel bear the names of rotten boroughs (Gatton near the middle, Old Sarum near the bottom). Underneath lies the discarded chaff, the corpses of the poor, and from the mill pours a stream of pensions, places and sinecures, which those in control of the boroughs greedily stuff into their pockets, while praising the system and opposing reform.

sends two county members, and so does the county of Rutland, which contains not an hundredth the part of that number. The town of Old Sarum, which contains not three houses, sends two members; and the town of Manchester, which contains upwards of sixty thousand souls, is
15 not admitted to send any. Is there any principle in these things? Is there anything by which you can trace the marks of freedom, or discover those of wisdom? ... In a city, such for instance as Bath, which contains between twenty and thirty thousand inhabitants, the right of electing representatives to Parliament is monopolized by about thirty-one per-
20 sons.

Another influential radical writer was John Wade, a working man who became a radical journalist. His *The Black Book; or Corruption Unmasked!* (1820) and its later version *The Extraordinary Black Book* (1832) were both bestsellers. They were compilations of data on the political system, which he and other radicals dubbed 'Old Corruption', showing the way aristocrats abused and exploited their influence by establishing sinecures and pensions for their followers. Wade claimed that the root of the evil was 'the corrupt state of the representation', especially rotten boroughs, and he demanded parliamentary reform.

Parliamentary reformers varied in their assumptions. Some, like Wade, were traditionalists (and poor historians!) who believed that, under the ancient Britons and Saxons, England had enjoyed a pure representative constitution, which had since been corrupted and largely destroyed. They thus demanded the restoration of lost rights, claiming that parliamentary reform was justified by historical precedents. Others, however, like Paine, argued from the inherent rights of man. Nevertheless, most reformers agreed that the system was insufficiently representative. Partly, they alleged, this was from the distribution of seats. Unimportant places were represented, while important ones were not; and, relative to population and importance, some areas had too many seats and others too few. Reformers especially condemned the rotten boroughs: Wade called them 'the cancer of the Constitution'. They criticised the franchises – especially corporation and burgage franchises – and insisted that not enough men could vote. They condemned electoral bribery, corruption, intimidation and disorder, and the high cost of electoral politics, which limited who could be candidates and so the electors' choice. They also criticised the statutory maximum duration of parliament (7 years) as giving electors insufficient control over MPs, and wanted a shorter period such as three years or even one.

Radicals criticised aristocrats' electoral patronage, alleging that peers had too much influence over constituencies and thereby over the House of Commons. Paine wrote that the House of Lords 'has obtained so much influence by borough-traffic, and so many of its relations and connections are distributed on both sides of the Commons, as to give it, besides an absolute negative in one House, a

preponderancy in the other in all matters of common concern'. Wade
alleged in his *Extraordinary Black Book* that the House of Commons
had become 'the mere organ of the Aristocracy'.

Finally, reformers agreed that the unreformed electoral system was
only part of the wider, evil system of exploitation and injustice in
Britain, and that the continuation of the former ensured that of the
latter. Wade claimed that the 'decayed boroughs' were the 'Pandora's
box, from which have flowed national calamities, desolating wars,
lavish expenditure, and monstrous debt'. Because of them 'all our
institutions are partial, oppressive and aristocratic'.

It followed from their argument that reform of the electoral system
would produce benefits for the whole of British life, including social
and economic improvements, as well as political. Radicals believed
that parliamentary reform could be the beginning of a golden age.

5 Contemporary Defences of the System

> **KEY ISSUE** What arguments were deployed to defend the existing
> arrangements?

Especially from the time of the French Revolution, conservative politicians and those who profited from the unreformed system
responded to the critics. They argued that the system did not need
reform, that the radical criticisms were fallacious and that change
would be harmful.

Some conservative propagandists were little concerned with logic
in defending the existing system. Mrs Hannah More, for instance,
wrote a series of cautionary tales for the poor, including *Village Politics*
(1792) (of which she wrote privately that it was 'as vulgar as heart can
wish; but it is only intended for the most vulgar class of readers'). Her
message was that the poor should be humble, sober and industrious,
revering the British Constitution, hating the French, and trusting in
God and in the goodwill of the gentry. Distributed free or selling in
vast quantities, her works undoubtedly reached far more people than
did Paine and the radicals.

Other conservatives claimed that the existing system worked well
and was justified by its results, especially prosperity, progress and victory in the wars against Napoleon. It protected liberty and property
and enabled the natural and best people, namely the aristocracy, to
rule, while also allowing other interests – including manufacturers
and merchants – some representation in the Commons. Even those
who were not themselves directly represented nevertheless were 'virtually represented': according to this view, MPs acted as the representatives not only of their electors but of the entire nation. At the
heart of their philosophy was the simple argument: why meddle with

something that was working well? Why turn to untried, and therefore potentially dangerous, experiments? Equally, why follow reforms which were proving unsuccessful elsewhere? British conservatives were quick to point out that the French Revolution, with its proud promises of 'liberty, equality and fraternity', had degenerated into the 'Reign of Terror' and the military dictatorship of Napoleon. Better, therefore, to bear those ills Britons had than to fly to others that might prove appreciably worse. Critics of the system were dubbed unpatriotic adherents of 'French principles' which were alien to the English spirit.

Some conservatives admitted that the system was not perfect but insisted that perfection could not exist this side of the grave. Others were bolder, claiming that even the alleged abuses of the system worked to its advantage. Royal and aristocratic influence at elections was said to help prevent conflict between the Lords and Commons and so to produce harmonious administration. Similarly, rotten boroughs helped produce stable government and provided the means for outstanding politicians (like the elder Pitt, MP for Old Sarum, who presided over the expansion of the British Empire in the eighteenth century) to enter parliament. And if some major towns were not directly represented, they were at least saved all the trouble and expense of elections.

The most influential conservative writer was the politician Edmund Burke, whose *Reflections on the Revolution in France* (1790) sold thousands of copies and profoundly influenced the propertied classes. It was he who gave intellectual respectability to the defence of the unreformed system. Burke summed up the more positive side of conservative thinking:

1 A state without the means of some change is without the means of its conservation ... We must all obey the great law of change ... All we can do, is to provide that the change shall proceed in insensible degrees ...
   Our constitution ... is a constitution, whose sole authority is, that it
5 has existed time out of mind ... It is a presumption in favour of any settled scheme of government against any untried project, that a nation has long flourished under it. It is a better presumption even of the choice of a nation, far better than any sudden and temporary arrangement by actual election ... The multitude, for the moment, is foolish, when they
10 act without deliberation; but the species is wise, and when time is given to it, as a species, it almost always acts right.

Defenders of the constitution often compared it to a living organism, capable of growth and adaptation: it had a life of its own with which reformers, whose rhetoric about natural or ancient rights was so much hot air, should not meddle. If unnatural reforms were introduced, the results could not be other than catastrophic. The balance of the constitution would be destroyed, so that the Commons would become too powerful. And if the vote were extended to the 'swinish multitude' and rule by the people ensued, the results would surely include violence, extended corruption, anarchy, terror, the destruction of religion, war and probably an eventual military dictatorship.

6 Conclusion

> **KEY ISSUES** Why is it so difficult to formulate an overall judgement on the unreformed political system?

a) Historical Interpretations

Until recently most historians interpreted the unreformed electoral system in a similar way to the contemporary critics. They judged that it was essentially unrepresentative and corrupt; that the small electorate was bribed or intimidated into voting as the upper classes wanted; and that therefore the 1832 Reform Act was a necessary and immense improvement. Yet in the 1980s and 1990s this 'Whig' interpretation (see page 6) has been challenged by revisionist historians, notably O'Gorman and Phillips (see Further Reading on page 151), who have made detailed studies – based largely on computer processed data from pollbooks and other sources – of samples of borough constituencies. They allege that earlier historians were far too much influenced by radical reformers' propaganda and so misrepresented the system and exaggerated its faults. Phillips alleges that previous historians 'denigrated or ignored' the unreformed electorate, and O'Gorman insists that they were 'morbidly preoccupied with the unsavoury aspects' of pre-1832 politics, adding that his purpose was 'to rescue the unreformed electorate from the Whig interpretation of English history', which he sees as a 'grotesque distortion of the truth'. The revisionists have argued that the electoral system was more representative and participatory, and less corrupt, deferential and dominated from above, than had previously been thought – that it was essentially not 'Old Corruption' but rather 'Old Vitality'.

The research carried out by Phillips and O'Gorman is so detailed, and based so squarely on primary evidence, that many have found it authoritative. The problem lies in its scope. Phillips first studied four boroughs from 1761 to 1802 and subsequently seven boroughs from 1818 to 1841; O'Gorman's core sample was six boroughs. The crucial issue is the sample and its relationship to the wider system. How typical and therefore how representative were their chosen constituencies? The revisionists have worked mostly on the boroughs. This is understandable, given their need to select constituencies which had regularly contested elections and which had electorates which were not so large as to be unmanageable. Yet though there were more borough than county seats, there were more county than borough voters. The 'typical' voter, if this concept has any validity, was therefore not a borough voter but a 40-shilling freeholder in the counties – and Phillips and O'Gorman have largely ignored him. Nor does it seem likely that their sample of seats was representative even of the boroughs, given that the unreformed system was so varied, containing a total of 202 boroughs in England alone. Many boroughs had much smaller electorates and far fewer contested elections than those examined by the revisionists, whose findings may therefore be atypical of the system as a whole.

All subsequent historians will be in the debt of the revisionists for their detailed scholarly contribution to the study of parts of unreformed politics, but further research is still needed before we may judge the whole system with any degree of certainty. And since so many poll books have not survived, all verdicts should be cautious.

b) Verdict

Much has been written against the unreformed system. It was undemocratic, excluding from voting the majority of the population, including all women, most working-class men and many middle-class men. Its distribution of seats was inadequately representative and excluded important towns. It included rotten boroughs, of varying types and degrees of rottenness, as well as the occasional sale of seats, corruption, bribery, intimidation, violence and plural voting. It was dominated by the aristocracy and gentry, and many seats were uncontested. Electors had limited choice, and certainly the majority of the population was excluded, largely by the expense, from standing as candidates. Nevertheless, as the revisionists have emphasised, there was also much that can be cited in defence of the system and especially the extent to which, despite its faults and limitations, it was flexible, participatory and representative. The verdict on the unreformed electoral system should therefore be a mixed one, though this is not to say equal weight should be given to its positive and negative features.

The system was so varied that there is much truth in the writings of both its critics and its defenders, and of both 'Whig' and revisionist historians. Some boroughs were so 'rotten' that they represented only their patron, while others saw active electoral contests in which a wide proportion of the population took part.

Participation and a form of representation were undoubtedly features of the unreformed system, and exceptionally, as in 1830–2 (see page 42), the electorate could significantly influence government action. But on the whole, as contemporaries well knew, it was heavily dominated by the aristocracy and the gentry, especially the former. The landed interest almost monopolised power. Even O'Gorman has written of the ability of the elite 'in the last analysis, to control the electorate'. The popular participation so expertly researched by the revisionists may have been little more than a charade, hardly masking the continued reality of aristocratic power.

Perhaps the major difficulty in summing up the unreformed electoral system is one of values. We may be all too liable, from our present-day perspective, to condemn conventions and practices which at the time were generally accepted as normal. For instance, 'treating' was accepted by nearly everyone and was not considered corrupt. Nor was the buying and selling of constituencies considered reprehensible by all, and the great majority of those with wealth looked upon 'democracy' or 'universal suffrage' as evils to be avoided. But perhaps the key to understanding the first third of the nineteenth century lies in the fact that political assumptions were changing quite rapidly.

Radicals such as Paine had articulated alternative political philosophies, based not on property and hereditary right but on the 'natural rights' of all, throwing the defenders of the established system on to the defensive. In addition, industrialisation and urbanisation were beginning to affect Britain significantly. Population growth and movement, together with the generation of new wealth, were making a political system which many had considered effective in the past look increasingly anachronistic. At the start of the 1830s battle-lines were joined. The system was no longer nearly so representative of wealth and power in Britain, and the forces demanding a redistribution of power were growing. Some form of change seemed virtually certain sooner or later: the key questions concerned timing and extent. Many insisted that the alternatives were not the status quo or reform but reform or revolution.

Summary Diagram
The Unreformed Political System

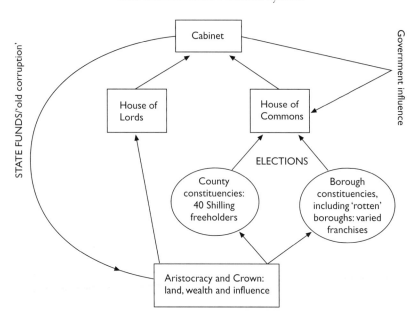

Your notes should enable you to understand the nature of the electoral system before 1832 and the various ways in which contemporaries criticised and defended it. These issues are important in themselves and provide an essential background for an understanding of the reforms dealt with in the next two chapters. The headings and sub-headings should enable you to organise your notes conveniently.

You will no doubt have realised by this stage that the pre-1832 electoral system is immensely complicated: your notes need to express this complexity without themselves becoming disjointed. The study diagram should help; and indeed you might experiment with making notes in 'pattern' form rather than in continuous prose. The degree of detail that you include should be designed to suit your particular needs: better to have brief notes which are clear and comprehensible than a comprehensive set which will confuse. A good idea might be to compile two sets. The first, simple and brief, should focus on structure; then, when you are happy with this set, you might venture into greater depth. Pay particular attention to the Conclusion. There is scope here for you to try to formulate your own overall generalisations.

Answering structured and essay questions on Chapter 2

A typical structured question is:

1. a) What features of the unreformed political system did radical critics attack, and why? (5 marks)
b) How did conservatives defend the system against its critics? (5 marks)
c) How likely was it that the old system could continue unchanged in the nineteenth century? (10 marks)

Often the first parts of a structured question at AS level require straightforward factual answers. If you have read the contents of this chapter, you should have little trouble answering the first two parts of the above title. But do be aware of how many marks are available, and tailor your answers accordingly. Deal with the main criticisms and the main defences, and do so directly. It is in the third part that you can be more reflective. Here you should build on the information provided in (a) and (b) to argue your own case. Did the critics or the defenders of the existing system get the better of the arguments, and how much support might each side be able to muster? Equally important, did the changes that were occurring in Britain – stemming from industrial growth – tend to favour one side of the other?

Structured questions, by encouraging you to build an argument squarely upon a body of factual evidence, should be ideal preparation for tackling the more demanding A2-level essay questions. Examples of these include the following:

1. 'A system in crying need of urgent and substantial reform.' Discuss this view of the electoral system around 1830.
2. In what ways, and with what success, did the defenders of the pre-1832 political system argue that reform was unnecessary?

For each of these questions you should try to construct an essay plan. An essay should always be planned, rather than simply written without preparation, and therefore all students need a lot of practice at this invaluable skill. In general, an essay plan should involve: (i) an introductory paragraph in which you analyse the meaning of the title and in which you establish which areas (or sub-divisions of the question) you need to address later in the essay; you should also outline the argument you will adopt or, alternatively, several possible interpretations which you will compare. (ii) a list of the paragraphs which will form the body of the essay: remember that a paragraph should focus on one relevant aspect of the question, and one only. You can have two paragraphs on a particularly important issue, but do not deal with several issues in the same paragraph, otherwise your work is likely to become too complicated and its meaning lost. You should establish the relevance of each paragraph's issue or theme explicitly: don't leave it to the marker to realise in what ways it is relevant. Each paragraph should also contain illustrations and examples, i.e. evidence to support the point you are making, but these need not be included in an essay plan, unless you are doing a particularly full plan. (Nevertheless, do remember that evidence is vital: an essay should never consist solely of unsubstantiated generalisations. For AS level you can have paragraphs solely of information; but for A level you need to integrate the facts into your argument). (iii) a conclusion, in which you hammer home your answer to the question set as directly as possible. Do not introduce new material at this stage: simply sum up your argument and, perhaps, draw out its implications.

If you draw up an essay plan of this type, you are half-way to writing a good answer. Above all, you will avoid the most common fault – giving a narrative, or simply describing issues and events, on the general topic. Instead, you have to answer the precise question set. A good history essay should be a relevant analysis in which you argue a case by drawing upon a thoughtful selection of details, examples and illustrations.

Now try to construct essay plans for the two questions above. The first is relatively open-ended: you are merely asked to discuss a particular view of the unreformed system. In your opening paragraph you might mention the controversy between the opponents and defenders of this system, and in the conclusion you are free to give your particular verdict on pre-1832 politics. But which areas will form the material for the middle paragraphs? Draw up a list of half a dozen, remembering that they should form discrete areas. Next, construct a plan for the second title. This is less open-ended. You will need to define 'success' in your opening paragraph, and return to this issue in your conclusion. Perhaps the 'ways' in which the system was defended might form successive paragraphs in the body of the essay. You will, no doubt, cover the arguments used in defence of the system. Can you think of any other paragraphs? Perhaps Burke is so important that he deserves a paragraph to himself? You might also draw attention to the tactics used by the anti-reformers in 1831–2 – which are covered in chapter 3 – so interpreting 'ways' more widely than as 'intellectual arguments'.

Source-based questions on Chapter 2

1. The nomination ceremony and Dickens's Eatanswill election

Read the extracts from the journalist and from Charles Dickens on page 16, and then answer the following questions:

a) The account by the journalist is meant to be factual; but how convincing do you find it? Explain your answer fully. (*5 marks*)

b) Which aspects of the journalist's account are corroborated by Dickens? (*4 marks*)

c) Why do you think Dickens called his borough 'Eatanswill'? (*2 marks*)

d) Who were the 'Blues' and the 'Buffs' (lines 6–8)? Why do you think they were given such names? (*2 marks*)

e) What was the nature of the 'temporary dizziness of the head' (line 24)? (*2 marks*)

f) Why did the 'small body of electors' delay voting until the end of the election? (*4 marks*)

g) From your knowledge of the period, say how far you consider that the accounts by the journalist and by Dickens were typical of elections under the unreformed political system. (*6 marks*)

2. Paine's attack on and Burke's defence of the system

Read the extracts from Tom Paine and Edmund Burke on pages 18–20 and 22 and answer the following questions:

a) What did Paine mean when he described the franchise system as 'limited' and 'capricious' (lines 3 and 4)? (*2 marks*)

b) According to Paine (line 3), what percentage of the adult male population could vote? How accurate was his figure? (*2 marks*)

c) Paine gave the example of a wealthy farmer who could not vote (line 8). Explain why this individual would be ineligible for the franchise. (*2 marks*)

d) Does it seem, from the extract, that Paine favoured universal suffrage? Justify your answer. (*5 marks*)

e) Why did Burke believe that change should 'proceed in insensible degrees' (lines 3–4)? (*3 marks*)

f) Explain Burke's distinction between the 'multitude' and the 'species' (lines 10–13). (*3 marks*)

g) Do you find Paine or Burke the more convincing? Which were contemporaries likely to find the more persuasive? Explain your answers. (*8 marks*)

3 The Great Reform Act

POINTS TO CONSIDER

This chapter examines one of the most important pieces of legislation in nineteenth-century Britain, the Reform Act of 1832 – its origins, the provisions of the legislation and its impact. Whereas the content of the Act is a matter of fact, you have to make up your own mind on the highly controversial issues of why this legislation was passed and on what effects it had. Hence this chapter needs to be read in conjunction with Chapters 2 and 4, which provide important context.

KEY DATES

1821 Corrupt borough of Grampound was disfranchised.

1829 Catholic Emancipation, alienating the Ultras; economic slump; Attwood founded the Birmingham Political Union.

1830 (June) death of George IV, accession of William IV; (July–Sept.) general election, weakening Tories; (July) revolution in France; 'Swing' riots, continuing into 1831; (Nov.) Wellington resigned, Grey as PM.

1831 (May) Russell introduced reform bill in Commons; (April) defeat of reform bill, general election brings about Whig gains; (Oct) second reform bill defeated in Lords, riots in Bristol and elsewhere.

1832 (May) third reform bill defeated in Lords, 'Days of May'; (June) Reform Act.

In 1831 riots occurred in Bristol. Parts of the city were looted and burned, and afterwards the charred corpses of drunken rioters lay in the gutters. This was just one episode in the greatest political crisis of nineteenth-century Britain, the reform crisis of 1830–2, when the country seemed on the verge of revolution. The outcome was the 1832 Reform Act, the 'Great Reform Act', the first restructuring of Britain's electoral machinery in modern history. It was preceded by extensive and often bitter debates in parliament and has been followed by debates – certainly as extensive if not quite as bitter – between historians attempting to explain its causes and its significance.

1 Context and Causes of the Reform Crisis

KEY ISSUE Which groups supported political reform and why did they do so?

a) The Reform Movement

The origins of the electoral reform movement can be traced back as far as the seventeenth century, when the Levellers advocated manhood suffrage and urged that the representation accorded to an area should be proportionate to its population. But it was in the 1760s, in London, that the movement first started to achieve mass support. Then the example of the French Revolution of 1789 boosted demands for reform, even appealing to members of the opposition party, the Whigs; but, as French democratic idealism gave way to the 'Terror' and as Britain went to war with France, the authorities feared revolution and used repression in an attempt to stamp out new ideas. Reform was no longer respectable. There was renewed agitation in the years after 1815, when widespread unemployment and hardship attracted mass popular support to the reform movement. Improvements in economic conditions in the 1820s, however, led to a temporary lessening of reform fever.

There were different groups urging change. Radicals called for the most extensive reforms. Despite government persecution, radical publications – especially Paine's *Rights of Man* and a variety of journals – were widely distributed. There were insistent calls for universal manhood suffrage, as well as for annual elections, equal electoral districts, a secret ballot, the payment of MPs and for the abolition of the property qualification so that a greater variety of people might stand for parliament. Several outstanding individuals achieved a large following. Amongst these were William Cobbett, the son of a small farmer who became a journalist and attacked 'Old Corruption' in print, and Henry ('Orator') Hunt, the self-styled 'Champion of Liberty', a wealthy gentleman farmer who became a pugnacious and popular radical leader and consistently urged democratic parliamentary reform, including manhood suffrage. But no national organisation or leadership existed, and whereas some radicals based their ideas on Paine's belief in the natural rights of man, others looked backwards, insisting that there should be a return to the ancient rights of Englishmen. Alongside demands for a thoroughgoing cleansing of the electoral system came calls, from moderate radicals and Whigs, for more limited, reformist measures such as disfranchising the worst rotten boroughs and enfranchising some of the larger towns.

Why had the movement failed to achieve parliamentary reform by 1827? There are two main explanations. The first is that Tory governments (in office 1807–1830) opposed reform. Political parties were not as united or as well organised as they were later: many MPs refused to adopt either the 'Tory' or the 'Whig' label, and most governments had to be coalitions rather than single-party administrations. Nevertheless, of the two conventional alignments, it was the Tories who were the more powerful, and successive Tory governments had the backing of the monarchy and of the armed forces, an invaluable asset in times of strife. In short, the Tories were strong enough to resist the reformers. The pro-reform Whig peers and MPs, and the radical MPs, were a small minority and therefore powerless in parliament. Indeed the second major reason to explain the failure of reform is that its adherents had not achieved sufficient unity or support from Britain's population to win over the politicians. This is not to say, however, that they did not have significant numbers of supporters.

i) The Working Classes

The urban, industrial and mining working classes, which were growing rapidly in size from about 1780, had many grievances, including poverty, insecurity and poor working and living conditions. As a result, they were beginning to become conscious of themselves as an exploited class and so were becoming increasingly politically aware.

By 1820 the radicals had won massive working-class support for parliamentary reform. Though active allegiance varied and tended to die down when the economic situation improved, fluctuating broadly in line with the price of bread, it still continued. Working-class support was due mostly to the idea that from the reform of parliament would arise much-needed social and economic improvements. To the question whether the reform of parliament would 'give the labouring man a cow or a pig ... put bread and cheese into his satchel instead of infernal cold potatoes ... give him a bottle of beer to carry to the field instead of making him lie down upon his belly to drink out of the brook', Cobbett answered that 'it would do them all'.

ii) Dissenters

Numerous among the middle and working classes, and with strong feelings of identity, were the Dissenters. These were the Protestants outside the established Church of England, including Presbyterians, Baptists, Quakers and others. In the late-eighteenth and early-nineteenth centuries they were growing rapidly in numbers. Indeed, by 1820 they may have constituted 30 per cent of the population, and in some towns they were the majority. They were especially strong in the industrial midlands and north, where they included leading merchants, bankers and industrialists. Their grievances stemmed from the fact that they were denied full civil rights, being excluded from corporations, universities and some state offices, while in addition they – like everyone else – were taxed to support the Established Church. Hence they wanted parliamentary reform so that they would be better represented and have the chance to remove their disabilities. Certainly they provided substantial support for the reform movement. It was later stated in parliament that they had been 'the life of the agitation' for the Reform Bill.

iii) The Industrial and Commercial Middle Classes

With industrialisation and increasing trade, the urban middle classes were growing in numbers, wealth and importance, and – partly through the newspaper and periodical press – in economic and political awareness as well. They certainly did not all share the same political views, but many of them were becoming disillusioned with the unreformed system. Increasingly they felt that it failed to represent and protect their interests, and that it enabled an aristocratic parliament and government to get away with mismanaging the nation's affairs. Although their own wealth was increasing in this period, many industrialists and merchants believed that government policies, made by landed aristocrats, were harmful both to their interests and to the economy as a whole. For example, the middle classes greatly resented the Corn Laws of 1815, which stopped foreign grain entering Britain until prices within the country were very high. This was considered to be very much in the interests of landowners, since it was thought to keep up the domestic price of wheat (although historians now doubt whether the Corn Laws had any such effect), but high bread prices seemed counter to the national interest as a whole. There was also resentment at the exclusion of many middle-class men from the borough franchise and at the non-representation of industrial towns such as Birmingham and Manchester, and with them of important economic interests such as cotton manufacture. A substantial number of middle-class men therefore supported the movement for parliamentary reform.

Middle-class hostility to the unreformed system was reinforced by Jeremy Bentham's philosophy of Utilitarianism. Bentham was not a politician but his ideas were considered by many to be relevant to politics. He believed that institutions should be judged not by abstract principles or historical precedents but by whether or not they produced 'the greatest happiness of the greatest number'. He argued that parliament should therefore be efficient, unwasteful and of benefit not just to small numbers but to as many people as possible; and if it was not – and clearly the unreformed system left great numbers dissatisfied – then it should be reformed accordingly.

Thus there were substantial reasons why the middle classes should support reform. But alongside their discontents and hopes existed fear. Businessmen, industrialists and professionals were generally men of substance, men with much to lose. The last thing they wanted was a violent revolution, with all the destruction that would accompany it. Scarcely more appealing was the radical programme of universal suffrage. The working and middle classes might be united by a common dissatisfaction with the existing system, but they had different ideas about what should replace it. The middle classes wanted the enfranchisement of men like themselves, 'responsible citizens' who owned property and thus had an economic stake in the country; but if the vote were to be extended to all men, then the larger size of the working classes would ensure that they gained control of the state and the economy.

b) The Reform Movement by 1827

The reform movement had achieved a firm foundation by 1827. It had spread the idea of parliamentary reform, the arguments for it (including criticisms of the unreformed system) and the data to support those arguments, especially through the works of Paine and Wade (see pages 18–21). The movement had publicised the abuses and anomalies of the unreformed system – making rotten boroughs such as Old Sarum and Gatton notorious – and had made parliamentary reform an important and persistent political issue. Probably a large majority of the population wished there to be some measure of reform.

There seemed to be no real threat of violent revolution around this time, and so the government could no longer turn to repression to stem the tide of new and unwelcome political ideas. Indeed parliament agreed in 1821 to disfranchise the corrupt Cornish borough of Grampound and allot its two seats to Yorkshire, a limited measure which whetted the reformers' appetite for more. In this new atmosphere, parliamentary reform seemed a much more respectable and realistic political goal for the middle classes. Working-class and middle-class dissenters formed a fairly unified group: the key question was whether the middle and working classes as a whole could work together in some way to campaign for reform. If they could, it would be very difficult to resist their combined pressure.

Yet in 1827 the Tories were firmly in control and saw little realistic prospect of parliamentary reform being thrust upon them in the near future. They believed that the middle classes' fear of democracy would be greater than their dissatisfaction with the unreformed system, and they were confident of their own ability to weather any storm. They were to be profoundly shocked by the severity of the squalls over the next few years.

2 The Disintegration of Tory Hegemony, 1827–9

> **KEY ISSUE** What factors combined to weaken the Tories?

Several factors combined to weaken the Tories. One was complacency. They had been in office for 20 years and assumed that they would be in for at least another 20. After all, the parliamentary Whigs and radical opposition were numerically weak and there was no longer war abroad or the threat of revolutionary agitation at home. Another factor was the resignation from illness in February 1827 of Lord Liverpool, who has been described as 'the most underrated prime minister of the century'. A shrewd and competent politician,

Liverpool had helped to keep the Tories together. His resignation was followed by a period of political uncertainty, fluidity and partial realignment. In 1827–8 the Tories split between the more conservative majority, led by the Duke of Wellington and Robert Peel, and a minority of 'Liberal Tories'.

In 1828 Wellington emerged as party leader and prime minister. The hero of Waterloo had been a great military commander, but he lacked political skill and, partly because of deafness (caused by standing too near an explosion), was insufficiently aware of shifting political realities. He aimed to reunite the Tories and prevent parliamentary reform, but in fact his premiership was to have the opposite results. Immediately several talented Liberal Tories resigned from his government, and later that year an even more important fracture of the party occurred over Catholic Emancipation (the abolition of the old laws which prevented Catholics from becoming MPs and holding certain other positions).

In 1828 the Irish Catholic leader Daniel O'Connell won a by-election in Ireland, thereby precipitating a major crisis for the new government. As a Catholic, O'Connell was not eligible to become an MP, and yet his exclusion would be certain to infuriate the Catholic majority in Ireland. Wellington had previously opposed Catholic Emancipation and still did not want it, but now he believed it was a necessary evil. The alternative might well be civil war in Ireland. In 1829 a law allowing Catholics to become MPs was passed with Whig and radical support.

Catholic Emancipation further divided and weakened the Tories. In particular it alienated the Protestant right-wing Tories, known as the Ultras. They had recently accepted the government's repeal of laws discriminating against Dissenters only with great reluctance, but Catholic Emancipation was too much for them to swallow. Believing that Wellington and Peel had 'ratted' and betrayed their principles, the Ultras opposed the Tory government. Moreover they changed their attitude towards parliamentary reform, to which they had previously been hotly opposed. They now reasoned that since Catholic Emancipation had been unpopular in the country, a more representative electoral system – particularly without the rotten boroughs – would have thrown it out. In this way the most unlikely group of all – those at the extreme right of the Tory Party – had been converted into parliamentary reformers.

One of the major obstacles to parliamentary reform had long been the power of the anti-reform Tory government. Now, at the end of the 1820s, the Tories had splintered. This itself cannot be said to have caused parliamentary reform, but it certainly made it a more feasible political prospect.

3 The Reform Crisis, 1830–2

> **KEY ISSUES** What short-term and long-term causes explain the introduction and the passing of the 1832 Reform Bill? What were the intentions of the Whigs in introducing it, and what fears motivated those who opposed it?

a) Political Unions and the Revival of Reform

In the early-nineteenth century popular discontent and popular politics were closely related to the state of the economy. In 1829 and 1830 poor harvests and economic slump caused higher bread prices, unemployment and distress for many in the working classes, together with losses, failures and anxiety for businessmen.

Partly in response to this, the parliamentary reform movement was revived by veterans like Hunt and Cobbett. Furthermore, at the end of 1829 Thomas Attwood, a Birmingham banker, founded a parliamentary reform organisation and pressure-group, a 'General Political Union between the Lower and Middle Classes of the People', usually known as the Birmingham Political Union, which became the model for others formed elsewhere in the country in 1829–30. Their composition varied with local circumstances; but in many places, as in Birmingham, the unions saw massive co-operation between the middle and working classes. The slump was thus drawing together diverse critics of the unreformed system in a new challenge to the Tories. The class alliance which the Tories feared seemed to be coming about.

b) King William IV and the 1830 Election

In June 1830 King George IV died and was succeeded by his brother, who became William IV. This had important political repercussions and was one of the factors contributing to parliamentary reform. It ended the reign of a man who was passionately devoted to the Tories and loathed the Whigs, and it produced a general election (as was customary on the death of a monarch) whose results further weakened the Tories. In fact, the election was inconclusive and confusing, with no party gaining a majority. But the government lost support in the counties and open boroughs – in those constituencies where public opinion counted for most – and the trend was definitely against the Tories and in favour of parliamentary reform. The government still had more MPs than the opposition groups, but the balance was held by over 200 MPs whose allegiance was doubtful. Wellington's government could continue in office, but for how long was uncertain.

c) Reform, 'Swing' and Wellington's Fall, 1830

The reform movement continued to gain support. The reformers were encouraged by the July revolution in France, which overthrew the reactionary Bourbon monarchy, and by the election results, especially by the return of the reformer Henry Brougham (pronounced 'Broom') as one of the members for the county of Yorkshire. Brougham was a brilliant Scottish lawyer who had promised to initiate parliamentary reform. Almost certainly, he was better known and more popular in the country than any of the Whig leaders.

In 1830, while the reform movement grew but entirely separate from it, the 'Swing riots' (named after an imaginary 'Captain Swing' who was said to lead the movement) occurred in the rural southern counties of England. These involved the burning of hayricks and attacks by impoverished and desperate farm workers on threshing machines, which they blamed for reducing their employment. They were apolitical, spontaneous and uncoordinated, and they were easily suppressed by the government. Nevertheless, they much alarmed the ruling classes, especially since agricultural labourers had previously seemed among the most docile of British workers. The unrest continued for over twelve months, providing a disturbing backdrop to events in parliament.

In November 1830 the Whigs, worried by all the unrest and encouraged by the opportunity resulting from the Tory decline, took the political initiative. The key figure was their leader, Earl Grey. Alone among the opposition politicians he had the experience, prestige and parliamentary following to make him a potential prime minister. He had championed reform as early as the 1790s, but now he was slow to act, and did so only under pressure from the younger Whigs and because of his alarm that, unless decisive and appropriate action were taken, the unrest would escalate, possibly into a revolution. While Wellington continued to profess, somewhat fatuously, that the existing system 'possessed the full and entire confidence of the country', Grey announced his intention to arrange for reform legislation to be introduced in the Commons. He thus threw down a gauntlet to Prime Minister Wellington.

Round one of the contest went to Grey. In November the Whigs, aided by radicals and former Tory supporters, Ultras and the Liberal Tories, defeated the government in the Commons, whereupon Wellington resigned, bringing to an end more than 20 years of Tory rule. Round two also went to the Whigs. Grey managed to form a government and so became premier later that month. Yet this was not the end of the reform contest. Although generally referred to as a Whig administration, his government was essentially a precarious coalition of several insecure alignments, and there was therefore no guarantee that it would survive in what seemed likely to be a long and bruising contest.

d) Grey's Reform Intentions

One of the government's first priorities was parliamentary reform. It hoped to introduce legislation quickly and so end the crisis. But it was not easy to agree on the contents of a bill. Some ministers were more radical than others, and there had to be extensive debates in cabinet before agreed measures could be placed before parliament.

Clearly a reform bill would have to remove the worst abuses of the old system. That meant, at the very least, (a) getting rid of the rotten boroughs, (b) providing parliamentary seats for rising towns which were not boroughs, and (c) providing a uniform borough franchise in place of the old multiple, and confusing, arrangements. But what should be the qualifications for the franchise? And how many people would be enfranchised by whatever proposal was made? The Whigs certainly had no intention of accepting radical proposals for universal male suffrage, but they found it hard to decide either where to draw the line or how to estimate the effects of particular franchise reforms.

Grey and his ministers were definitely not revolutionaries. They had no wish to introduce democracy, which they believed was likely to have calamitous consequences. Instead, they wished the government of Britain to continue to be carried out by aristocrats and landowners, men like themselves, with a leavening from the middle classes. Their aim was thus to modify and 'purify' the system, in order that it should survive. Grey instructed his draughtsmen to produce: 'a measure ... large enough to satisfy public opinion and to afford sure ground of resistance to further innovation, yet so based on property, and on existing franchises and territorial divisions, as to run no risk of overthrowing the [existing] form of government'.

Grey and the Whigs were reformers, but moderate ones. They wanted to change the old system, removing its most blatant abuses, and yet at the same time to preserve as much as possible of the social, political and constitutional status quo. Hence they were adamant that the franchise should be based on property, not on any inherent rights of man. Their strategy was to remedy the grievances of the middle classes, and so gain their support, but not those of the working classes. In this way they hoped to divide and rule, detaching middle-class men from the reform movement and leaving an isolated – and thus impotent – working class. The result would be a new alliance between the aristocracy and the middle classes, who together would form an impenetrable barrier to revolution and even to further constitutional change. In this way, the Whigs hoped to achieve a permanent settlement to the whole issue of parliamentary reform. In addition, they were motivated by party-political self-interest, reasoning that a government that enfranchised new voters would earn their gratitude in the form of their votes. The reform bill was thus designed to harm the Tories and benefit the Whigs.

The Whig government had no intention of satisfying the aspirations of those radicals and members of the working classes who optimistically saw a reform bill not as a minor and final change but as the beginning of a process which would improve their lives and bring about a new and better Britain. In the *Extraordinary Black Book* (1832), John Wade claimed that 'For the interests of the *few* the Reform Bill would substitute the interests of the *many* ... government would be founded on Public Opinion ... Cheap government – cheap bread – cheap justice – and industry unfettered and productive will reward our efforts in the triumph of the Reform Bill!' These were the sorts of hopes and expectations, fuelling mass support for the Bill throughout the reform crisis, which the government was intending to frustrate.

e) The First Reform Bill: Introduction and Debates

The Bill – the first of three to be introduced before one eventually became law – resulted from compromises between radical and conservative ministers. Its terms were kept secret until it was introduced in the House of Commons by Lord John Russell on 1 March 1831. According to a report of his speech, he argued as follows:

1 No doubt, at that very early period, the House of Commons did represent the people of England but ... the House of Commons, as it presently subsists, does not represent the people of England ... The people called loudly for reform, saying that whatever good existed in the con-
5 stitution of this House – whatever confidence was placed in it by the people, was completely gone ... and so long as towns like Leeds and Manchester elected no representatives, while such places as Gatton and Old Sarum did, it was impossible to say that the representation was fairly and properly carried on ...
10 His Lordship then stated the plan by which ministers proposed to meet and satisfy the demand for reform which they averred themselves to believe could no longer be resisted. That plan had been so framed as to remove the reasonable complaints of the people, and these complaints were principally directed, first, against nomination by individuals;
15 secondly, election by close corporations; thirdly, the expenses of elections ...

The Bill amazed MPs by its scope, being much more radical than they had expected. The diarist Charles Greville called it 'a sweeping measure indeed!' which produced massive excitement: 'Nothing talked of, thought of, dreamt of, but Reform'.

From then on until June 1832 there was a prolonged and sometimes violent crisis. It was driven by extra-parliamentary pressure from the political unions and other reform organisations. It was expressed by petitions on a massive scale, by demonstrations, riots and the threat of further disturbances. The Whig ministers were convinced of the strength of the public demand, which they believed made reform a necessity, and the more reluctant reformers justified their support on the basis that the people demanded it. All Whigs insisted that, if the Bill were not passed, there would be further disorder and possibly revolution, whereas its enactment would end the crisis, restore peace and stability, and preserve the constitution, monarchy and aristocracy.

The Tories refused to compromise and strongly opposed the Bill. They repeated the old arguments in favour of the unreformed system (see page 21), insisting that it did not need reform, that unenfranchised towns and persons were 'virtually' represented and that rotten boroughs provided seats for distinguished politicians and were necessary for stable government. Existing franchises produced a diverse electorate, whereas uniform qualifications would produce less variety. They also denied that there was mass public demand for change. Finally, they warned of the dire long-term consequences of the Bill, including the ending of the monarchy, aristocracy and Established Church. Peel later said, 'I was unwilling to open a door which I saw no prospect of being able to close.'

The Tory speakers included Sir Robert Inglis, who argued on 1 March 1831, the day the Bill was introduced, that

1 This House is not a collection of deputies ... We are not sent here day by day to represent the opinions of our constituents ... We are sent here to legislate, not for the wishes of any set of men, but for the wants and the rights of all ... If our conduct there be error, our constituents
5 have their remedy at a dissolution ...
Our constitution is not the work of a code-maker; it is the growth of time and events beyond the design or the calculation of man: it is not a building, but a tree ... Such, generally speaking, as the House of Commons is now, such it has been for a long succession of years: it is
10 the most complete representation of the interests of the people ... which comprehends within itself, those who can urge the wants and defend the claims of the landed, the commercial, the professional classes of the country; those who are bound to uphold the prerogatives of the Crown, the privileges of the nobility, the interests of the lower
15 classes, the rights and liberties of the whole people ... How far, under any other than the present circumstances, the rights of the distant dependencies, of the East Indies, of the West Indies, of the colonies, of the great corporations, of the commercial interests generally ... could find their just support in this House, I know not.

Outside parliament, radicals debated the Bill and soon changed their attitudes to it. They had wanted a reform bill, certainly, but this particular measure seemed far too moderate. Some denounced it as a selfish measure to enable the Whigs to gain middle-class support and alleged that it would not benefit the working classes. 'Orator' Hunt, for example, declared in a speech at Manchester that the government's policy was to get one million of the middle classes, the little shopkeepers and those people, to join the higher classes, in order to raise yeomanry corps and keep up standing armies, and thus unite together to keep their hands still in the pockets of the seven millions.

Others, especially middle-class radicals, argued that despite its faults it was a beginning which would lead to later reforms and so ultimately benefit the working classes. Most radicals supported the Bill – even Hunt finally voted for it on the grounds that at least it disfranchised the rotten boroughs – and their support was crucial to its passage.

f) Reform Crisis: Conflict and Victory

The reform legislation of 1831–2 was one of the most controversial measures in British political history. A prolonged and complex battle took place between the Whigs and Tories before the third version of the Bill eventually became law as the First Reform Act in 1832.

'Dame Partington and the Ocean'.

i) Grey versus Wellington

In March 1831 the Whigs won a debate on the First Reform Bill in the House of Commons by a single vote. However, their celebrations were premature, as the following month they were defeated on the issue. They persuaded the king to dissolve parliament and call a general election, which they won decisively by about 130 seats. Few MPs survived in the largest constituencies if they opposed reform. Public opinion was thus able to make itself felt even in the unreformed system. The Second Reform Bill was then accepted by the House of Commons, but to become an act it had also to receive the assent of the House of Lords, where there was a Tory majority. The Tory peers, led by Wellington who alleged that the Bill 'puts an end to aristocracy', defeated the Bill and precipitated a major crisis.

Wellington was depicted by a cartoonist as Dame Partington, the woman who had reputedly tried to keep Atlantic floods out of her seaside home with a mop (see the cartoon on page 41). Other protests were less subtle. The political unions organised demonstrations, while in Derby and Nottingham and elsewhere riots occurred, the most destructive taking place in Bristol. Fresh political unions sprang up. In the winter of 1831–2 further popular violence and even class war seemed possible, and some anxious peers and gentry fortified their country houses.

This agitation outside parliament strengthened the government in its determination. It introduced a third version of the Reform Bill, which passed the Commons but, in May 1832, was again defeated in the Lords. Grey's response was to ask the king to create another 50 Whig peers, to ensure the passage of the Bill, and when William IV refused, he resigned in protest. Wellington was then asked to try to form a new administration, amidst nationwide protests. Many contemporaries feared violent and bloody revolution in these 'Days of May'. The political unions held massive demonstrations and even threatened to form their own army. The reformers also used economic pressure. One London radical publicised the slogan 'To stop the Duke, go for gold', whereupon rich reformers started to withdraw gold coins from the banks in order to threaten a financial crisis.

Historians have debated the issue of whether Britain was indeed on the verge of revolution. Would the middle classes, who had so much to lose in any violent upheaval, really have made common cause with the workers, whom they were all too prone to dismiss as 'rabble'? Almost certainly there was an element of bluff in some of the forecasts of doom made by middle-class reformers, and the private papers of several Tory politicians reveal confidence that whatever violence occurred could be contained. But no one can be really sure what would have happened if reform had been much longer delayed, and almost certainly this was the closest Britain has come to a revolution during the last 300 years.

ii) Whig Victory

The issue was resolved not on the streets but in the Commons. Whigs and radical MPs refused to support a Tory government, and Wellington soon gave up his attempt to form an administration. Grey returned as prime minister and now the king agreed to create enough new peers to secure passage of the Bill, if the Lords rejected it once more. After Wellington's failure and the massive demonstrations of public opinion, the king had little choice but to acquiesce. The Duke decided to do the same. He and a majority of the Tory peers agreed not to oppose the Bill in the Lords. The contest between Whigs and Tories thus ended with the equivalent of a technical knock-out: the Tories threw in the towel. In June 1832, therefore, the Reform Bill finally passed, amidst massive public rejoicing and celebration. The long crisis was finally over. Separate, and very similar, Reform Acts were also passed in 1832 for Scotland and Ireland.

4 The 1832 Reform Act

> **KEY ISSUE** What were the provisions of the Act?

The Act was a complex measure. As Lord John Russell told the Commons in 1831, it was not based on 'perfect symmetry and regularity' and included many 'anomalies'. Nevertheless, its essential features are relatively straightforward. It omitted provision for a secret ballot or payment for MPs, it retained a property qualification for MPs and it maintained the maximum duration between elections at 7 years. Its essential reforms were to bring about a significant redistribution of seats and to simplify the franchise qualifications.

a) Redistribution

The total number of MPs in parliament remained the same (658). But the Act brought about important changes:

(i) It took seats from the smallest boroughs: 56 English boroughs (including the most notorious 'rotten boroughs') were disfranchised altogether, while another 30 lost 1 of their 2 MPs.

(ii) It extended the boundaries of many of the smaller boroughs to make them more populous and more viable representative units.

(iii) It created 22 new two-member parliamentary boroughs, notably in London, the industrial midlands, and the north. Birmingham, Manchester, Sheffield, Leeds and Bradford and other growing towns became parliamentary constituencies (each returning 2 MPs) for the first time.

(iv) It created 20 new single-member boroughs, including Gateshead and Kidderminster.

(v) In total, it redistributed 143 seats, over one-fifth of the total, to new parliamentary boroughs and to the counties.
(vi) It ended the traditional practice of allowing all counties 2 MPs, regardless of their size: 27 counties now gained another 2 MPs, while 7 more gained 1.
(vii) It took 18 seats from England and distributed them to other parts of the United Kingdom.

b) The Franchise: England and Wales

In the boroughs,

(i) there was to be a uniform franchise: all £10 householders (i.e. all male owners or occupiers of property worth £10 a year in rent) were eligible to vote, providing they had not been in receipt of poor relief over the previous year; and
(ii) in addition, pre-1832 franchise-holders kept their voting rights during their own lifetimes, providing they lived within 7 miles of the borough and it was still a constituency.

In the counties,

(iii) the old 40-shilling freeholder qualification continued;
(iv) in addition, the vote would go to adults leasing or renting land worth at least £50 per annum — the 'Chandos clause', named after the Tory peer who introduced it as an amendment to the Bill; and
(v) some leaseholders (holding property on a lease) and some copyholders (whose property was held by custom rather than formally owned) could also vote.

In both boroughs and counties, the right to vote was limited to adult men who were not peers, lunatics, criminals or revenue officers. Lastly, the Act specified that henceforth a register of electors was to be compiled for every constituency.

5 Results

> **KEY ISSUE** How did the Reform Act affect the electoral system and the reality of political power?

The terms of the 1832 legislation, complex though they are, seem straightforward in comparison with its effects on the parliamentary system. It had important but diverse results, both short- and long-term, causing changes but also leaving continuities with the unreformed system.

The Whig historians of Victorian England tended to emphasise – and praise – the Act's changes and benefits, and to echo the opinion of John Bright: 'it was a great Bill when it passed'. To them, it was a far-sighted and generous measure, symbolising Britain's political success in the nineteenth century – the achievement of peaceful and progressive change. They insisted that it brought the middle classes to power without violent revolution, in sharp contrast to continental Europe, whose countries were either politically backward, and still dominated by the aristocracy, or subject to violent revolutionary upheaval. Since 1945, however, interpretations have changed. Historians have emphasised the Act's limitations and the continuities with the unreformed system, including the continued domination of the aristocracy. One historian has called it 'a rescue operation on behalf of rank and property'. According to such views, the Act no longer deserves its customary 'Great' prefix.

Probably both schools of thought are right up to a point, but both have been guilty of exaggeration. Recent revisionist historians have shown the complexity and variety of the post-1832 system. But before we can judge the overall effects of the legislation on the parliamentary system, we need to scrutinise its particular results.

a) Redistribution

By disfranchising the rotten boroughs and redistributing seats, the Reform Act made the electoral system correspond more closely to the distribution of population and wealth in the country. It reduced the over-representation of the boroughs relative to the counties, of agriculture relative to industry, of the south relative to the north, and of England relative to the rest of the United Kingdom.

Yet it is important to recognise that though it reduced the maldistribution of seats, the redistribution effected in 1832 was too limited to come close to ending it altogether. Representation still did not correspond very closely to population distribution. The rural south of England continued to be over-represented relative to London and the industrial north, just as small towns were still over-represented in comparison with large towns and cities. The counties had more MPs than before: but, despite containing more than one-half of the population, they still had only one-third of the seats. England had just over half the population of the United Kingdom and yet returned almost three-quarters of its MPs. Scotland was still relatively under-represented, despite its electorate increasing by almost 1,500 per cent. In addition, many small boroughs remained, including five with electorates under 200, and the average borough electorate was still under 900. At the same time, there were several towns with populations exceeding 10,000 which were denied separate parliamentary representation.

b) Electorate

The Reform Act increased the borough, county and total electorate.

How much the electorate increased cannot be known because of inadequate records and plural voting. As a result, historians have disagreed in their estimates. Most have judged that, over the country as a whole, probably about 20 per cent of adult men could vote (1 in 5), around twice as many as in the old system. But O'Gorman estimates that the increase was about half that amount, relatively insignificant compared with the later reform acts. As yet general agreement has not been reached on which of these estimates is likely to be the more accurate. However, if we compare the number of people who actually voted before and after 1832, the increase may be as high as 500 per cent, a greater percentage increase than that caused by any of the later acts. In part this is testimony to the degree to which the reform crisis of 1830–2 increased political awareness. More significantly, it is certain that a greater number of constituencies saw contested elections after 1832. Between 1832 and 1867 probably about half of elections were contested, compared with less than a third in the corresponding period before 1832.

c) Political Power

i) Aristocracy

The Reform Act had been passed in the teeth of intense hostility from the House of Lords, the peers acquiescing only when the threat of the creation of a large number of Whig peers gave them no real choice. The Reform Act, therefore, undoubtedly increased the prestige and power of the House of Commons relative to the Lords, especially now that it was more representative of the people. The reforms also hurt the aristocracy since, by eliminating rotten boroughs, it reduced their influence in the House of Commons. Yet, despite these changes, there was also much continuity with the unreformed system. As the government intended, the system was modified, not transformed, and the aristocracy retained its overall domination of politics, even if its extent had been decreased somewhat.

As the Whigs intended, aristocrats continued to have great influence over election to the Commons. This was partly because of their power in the counties. The county electorate remained essentially the same, with the 40 shilling freeholders comprising about 70 per cent of voters, while the new 'Chandos clause' voters – about 20 per cent – were vulnerable and deferential to their landlords: tenants, dependent for their livelihood on the owners of their property, were not liable to run the risk of defying their wishes, at least not when voting continued to be public. Aristocratic domination was further cemented by the removal of many hard-to-control urban areas from county constituencies, and the survival of many smaller constituencies. Many boroughs continued to be controlled (or at least largely influenced) by aristocratic landowners. After 1832 there were probably about 50 of these proprietary (or 'pocket') boroughs left in existence. Following the first election under the new rules there were nearly 500 landed MPs in the Commons, drawing forth from Charles Greville the comment that 'a Reformed Parliament turns out to be very much like every other Parliament'. As late as the 1860s one-third of all MPs had aristocratic connections. Furthermore, aristocratic power was underlined by continued domination of the cabinet. For most of the period between 1832 and 1867 peers formed a majority of the cabinet, while the only non-aristocratic prime minister in this period was Sir Robert Peel, and he was a considerable landowner – even if his family's wealth originated from his father's activities as a manufacturer.

ii) Middle Classes
The £10 householder franchise made middle-class men the majority of the electorate. Shopkeepers replaced skilled craftsmen as the largest occupational group in the boroughs. In addition, more middle-class men became MPs, especially for the new urban and industrial constituencies. The Act certainly made the urban middle classes more politically powerful and influential than ever before. Yet in fact the middle classes did not gain political control, only a greater share of power: the dominant group in parliament and government remained the landed aristocracy. The Anti-Corn Law League (1839–46), the largest and most wealthy middle-class pressure group, despite a massive campaign in the constituencies, was unable to secure the election of more than a few MPs – so revealing the limits of middle-class power after 1832. Furthermore, most middle-class men were glad to gain the vote (and those with the requisite property could vote in several constituencies), but many were too concerned with their work, or with local government, to wish to enter national politics.

iii) Working Classes
The working classes did not gain the vote from the Act, despite their role in ensuring that it was passed. Most did not qualify because the £10 franchise – which in practice varied with house values – in most places excluded them. Some artisans, particularly in London, did qualify, but in the northern industrial towns such as Leeds the working classes were effectively excluded. At the Leeds election of 1832, an observer commented that 'the *people* do not live in £10 houses'. House prices in the newly enfranchised industrial towns tended to be low, thus ensuring that their electorates were remarkably small: in Birmingham, for example, only about 5 per cent of the population could vote, mostly middle-class men. Some workers, such as those in disfranchised boroughs, actually lost the vote as a result of the Act. After 1832 working-class voters were largely 'ancient right' (i.e. pre-1832) franchise holders and their number decreased as they moved or died. Small wonder, then, that the working classes felt betrayed by

the Reform Act and by the Whigs who were responsible for it, their resentment contributing to the growth in the later 1830s and 1840s of Chartism, another movement for parliamentary reform and for democracy.

d) Corruption

Partly because there was no secret ballot, there was still much corruption after 1832. Indeed it may even have increased, and the 1841 general election was notoriously corrupt. Between the 1832 and 1867 Reform Acts, two boroughs were disfranchised for corruption, but there was still fraud, intimidation, violence and sometimes rioting.

One of the government's declared intentions in 1832 had been to reduce the cost of elections. This the Act did not achieve: most elections continued to be very expensive, and 'treating' was still looked upon as indispensable in contested elections. This, with the property qualification and absence of pay for MPs, continued to limit MPs to the relatively wealthy or those who could obtain financial backing from patrons.

e) Registration and Constituency Politics

The 1832 Act stipulated that a register of electors should be drawn up for each constituency. This, alongside the increased number of people eligible to vote, contributed to the growth of local constituency parties, which became better organised and more efficient. Both of the major parties appointed professional agents to maximise the number of their supporters who registered to vote (and, by objections, to reduce the number of their opponent's supporters). The effects of this process varied from constituency to constituency, but in the boroughs as a whole it undoubtedly increased political awareness, partisanship and turnout.

f) Whig Gains

The Act benefited the Whigs, as they had intended. They gained electorally because the rotten boroughs had been mainly Tory and because the new £10 voters largely favoured them, as benefactors who had given them the vote. By strengthening the aristocracy in the counties, it also consolidated the position of the Whig magnates. Overall the system undoubtedly favoured the Whigs and was a major cause of their being in power for most of the period until the Second Reform Act (1867). Moreover, confirmed in power by the 1832 election, they were able to pass the Municipal Corporations Act of 1835 (see page 90), which reformed town government and, by ending the old corporations, electorally weakened the Tories.

6 Conclusion

> **KEY ISSUES** How is the controversy over the Reform Act best interpreted? What significance should be assigned to it?

a) Origins

There is considerable controversy over the origins of the 1832 Reform Act. Today most historians probably accept the 'concession' interpretation that the Bill was introduced as a timely reform to detach the middle classes from their working-class allies and so prevent extensive reform or even revolution. However, there are alternatives, one of which is the 'cure' interpretation proposed by the American historian D.C. Moore: he claims that large areas of the county constituencies had become urban and radical, or potentially radical, and therefore no longer deferential to the aristocracy, and that the Whigs wanted to cure this problem and so safeguard aristocratic domination. By making such areas into new parliamentary boroughs, separate from the counties, the Whigs were ensuring that the aristocracy could continue to dominate in non-urban, deferential seats. But most historians reject this hypothesis, arguing that Moore much exaggerates the urban penetration of the counties. It has also been pointed out that there is very little evidence that the Whig ministers had such aims in mind. But then, it is very difficult to be certain of the real motivations of the leading politicians.

Several factors were clearly involved in the drawing up of the Reform Bill and in its subsequent enactment. First there was mass extra-parliamentary pressure, and the consequent fear on the part of the Whigs that, unless reform came about, there would be continued riots or revolution. Alongside such fears existed a second motive, political opportunism: the Whigs undoubtedly hoped to gain the votes of those whom they enfranchised. Thirdly – and too easily forgotten – there were the Whig principles which included the advocacy of a freer and more representative system. Many politicians at Westminster felt that, although universal suffrage would be a disaster, the old system had too many anomalies to be allowed to continue. They believed that industrial growth and urbanisation had rendered the unreformed parliamentary system anachronistic.

Almost certainly, all three factors played a role in bringing about the Reform Act. But which was the most important – fear, calculation or principle? To answer such a question would require knowledge of the true motives of the leading political figures, which even they may not have been fully aware of. Or might we judge that industrialisation itself was the fundamental cause of political reform? Furthermore, a proper analysis of the causes of the Act requires due weight to be given to the propaganda of radicals such as Paine, the splintering of the Tory Party at the end of the 1820s, as well as to events outside Britain such as the revolution of 1830 in France. We may be certain that the debate on the origins of the Reform Act will long continue.

b) Results

The legislation ended the crisis, re-stabilised politics and detached the middle classes from their political alliance with the working classes. Specifically, it brought about a redistribution of parliamentary seats and extended the franchise to include most middle-class males in the towns. The Reform Act ended the worst abuses of the old system; and yet, to modern eyes, it looks very much a half-way house, preserving pocket boroughs and allowing corruption to fester for the want of a secret ballot. The Act may have fulfilled its framers' intentions, but it disappointed many of its more radical supporters. Overall judgements therefore depend very much on one's point of view and especially on whether one highlights the changes or the continuities. (Nor is it altogether easy to decide which is which. If the proportion of contested seats rose from around 30 to 50 per cent, as it did, should this be considered as change or continuity?)

A perfectly valid case can be made out for the Reform Act as a 'Great' measure, preventing revolution and reinvigorating the political system. Often seen as a first, and symbolic, breaching of the dam, it is said to have put Britain on the path of peaceful, democratic change. It can also be said to have had an important psychological impact. The very fact of reform triumphant over reaction changed political attitudes. The Tories had warned that the Act would 'open the floodgates of reform', and their fears were well founded. The Act began the long process of parliamentary reform which, in the twentieth century, resulted in an approximately democratic system. Once the door was opened, there was no prospect of closing it: Peel was right.

Yet the Act may, equally validly, be interpreted as a minor piece of legislation which tinkered around with the system and paralysed pressure for a more thoroughgoing reform. It may thus have delayed, rather than hastened, democracy in Britain. According to this view, the Tories were quite wrong. They prophesied that the Act would itself be revolutionary – that it would lead to the end of the monarchy and the aristocracy, the House of Lords and the Established Church. Yet the aristocracy retained its political predominance until the 1880s, and its wealth far longer. For at least 50 years after 1832 the Whig prophecies – that the Act would preserve the existing system – proved far more accurate than those of the Tories.

Grey's government was undoubtedly concerned to prevent democracy (in the sense of rule by the people); but we can see that the Act of 1832 formed part of a step-by-step process which resulted in universal suffrage within a century. (And if this seems a long time to us,

Grey and the Whigs – not to mention the Tories – would have viewed the prospect of extending the vote so quickly with consternation.) Either interpretation is valid, depending on which time perspective one adopts. This is the central ambiguity which makes it so difficult to assign a single significance to the Reform Act.

Summary Diagram
The Great Reform Act

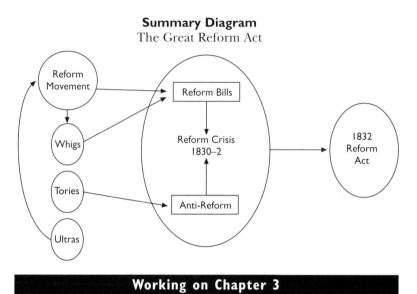

Working on Chapter 3

You need a full set of notes on this chapter, on the causes of reform, on the Act itself and on its consequences. The headings and sub-headings should help you to organise your notes satisfactorily. The concluding section is where you should try to grapple with the issues and set down your own views.

The least dramatic part of this chapter is, of course, the terms and provisions of the legislation. Do not be afraid to simplify the data given here (which itself is a simplification), but do so carefully. Be warned: it is all too easy to end up writing nonsense, as Seller and Yeatman did in *1066 And All That*. They described the main provision of this 'unforgettable Law' as follows:

1 householders leaseholders and copyholders who had £10 in the towns or freeholders who paid 40s in the country for 10 years or leaseholders (in the country) and copyholders for 21 years in the towns (paying a rent of £50) should in some cases (in the towns) have a vote (for 1
5 year) but in others for 41 years (in the country) paying a leasehold or copyhold of £10 should not.

Such an example shows the vital importance not only of punctuation, but of grasping the main features and principles of the Act, instead of merely attempting to learn its details.

Answering structured and essay questions on Chapter 3

The Great Reform Act is still an extremely popular exam topic. Here is a typical structured question;

1. **a)** What reforms of 'Old Corruption' did radicals like Paine wish to see enacted? (*10 marks*)
   b) What were the main reforms contained in the Great Reform Act regarding a) the franchise and b) the redistribution of seats? (*10 marks*)
   c) Why did the Great Reform Act prove so disappointing to radicals? (*20 marks*)

Students presented with c) as a complete essay question might well consider it daunting; but the structured question helps to 'demystify' essays. The most difficult task, if broken down into smaller steps, becomes manageable. (The way to tackle traditional essays is, of course, to break them down into smaller, easier parts.)

A-level questions generally focus on either the Act's origins or its impact. For the former, the following are typical:

1. 'Parliament was reformed in 1832 solely because of fear and political opportunism.' Do you agree?
2. How important was popular pressure in the passing of the Great Reform Act?
3. Why did attempts to reform parliament from 1815 not succeed until 1832?

Examples of the latter include:

4. Was the 1832 Reform Act 'the first major breach in the wall of privilege'?
5. Did the 1832 Parliamentary Reform Act fulfil its framers' intentions?
6. How significant were the changes brought about by the Reform Act of 1832?

Questions 1 and 2 are remarkably similar. Answers to both will include paragraphs on identical issues. But remember that the emphasis you give to an issue will depend partly on the wording of the question. For instance, in question 1 you must pay particular attention to the key issues of 'fear' (of what?) and 'political opportunism' (whose?). Even if you think that these two factors were not the vital ones leading to the Act, they are certainly vital in this particular question and therefore you must assess their importance very carefully. You will also have to bring in other factors, in order to see the two specified in the title in proper perspective, but you will probably spend less time on them. If you think other factors were important, then the answer in your conclusion must be 'No'. In question 2 you are directed to place one factor, 'popular pressure', in the context of other causes of the 1832 Act. Draw up a list of paragraphs for each of these two titles.

Try also to construct plans for questions 4–6. Remember the importance of defining the terms of each questions, especially since these definitions will often lead to the formulation of the relevant areas for subsequent paragraphs. Identification of the 'framers' intentions', in question 5, for instance, might well lead to subsequent paragraphs on each of them. Pay particular attention to question 6. This may seem relatively straightforward: all you have to do is to identify the major changes brought about by the Act and assess how important each one was and then how important they were as a whole. But be sure in each paragraph to *use*, rather than merely state, information. Perhaps you might start each paragraph with a judgement of one particular aspect of the reform (like the changes in the voting qualifications or the redistribution of seats, etc) and then bring in some factual information to support your statement. In this way, your argument will not be obscured by too many precise details. Remember, also, to deal with long-term as well as short-term consequences, and with intangible results, like the psychological fillip given to those who wanted to see peaceful change, as well as actual changes to the system.

Source-based questions on Chapter 3

1. *Lord John Russell and Sir Robert Inglis, for and against reform*

Read the speeches by Russell and Inglis on page 39 and 40, and answer the following questions:

a) How accurate were Russell's interpretation of the reforms 'the people' were calling for (line 4)? (*2 marks*)
b) What other complaints had been raised, besides the three Russell listed (lines 4–9)? (*3 marks*)
c) How might a reformer have responded to Inglis's arguments that MPs in the unreformed House of Commons legislated for 'the wants and rights of all' (line 4) and could be removed by their constituents (line 5)? (*5 marks*)
d) Explain how each man differed in his views on whether the House of Commons should 'represent' the people. (*10 marks*)
e) From your knowledge of the period, estimate which groups in the country would have supported each man's views. (*10 marks*)

4 Parliamentary Reform After 1832

POINTS TO CONSIDER

There were several measures of reform after 1832. Each one is important in itself, and you need to know what brought it about, what provisions it contained and what its effects were. You also have to judge whether the causes of these measures form any common pattern: if they do, you may be able to identify a driving force behind reform. Finally, you have to judge the cumulative significance of all the reforms.

KEY DATES

1864 Reform Union founded.
1865 Reform League founded; death of Palmerston; Russell PM and Gladstone Chancellor of the Exchequer.
1866 (June) defeat of Liberal Reform Bill; Derby's Conservative government, with Disraeli as Chancellor; (July) Hyde Park riots.
1867 Disraeli's reform bill became the Second Reform Act.
1872 Ballot Act: secret voting.
1883 Corrupt and Illegal Practices Act: election corruption penalised.
1884 Franchise Act, extending county franchise.
1885 Redistribution Act, producing mostly single member constituencies.
1897 National Union of Women' Suffrage Societies (Millicent Fawcett).
1897 Women's Social and Political Union (the Pankhursts).
1911 Payment for MPs (£400 per annum).
1918 (Feb.) Representation of the People Act ('Fourth Reform Act'): votes for men at 21 and qualified women at 30; maximum of 2 plural votes; elections to be held on a single day.

The legislation of 1832 did not open the floodgates to electoral reform. Indeed for a quarter of a century there were no further reform bills, despite popular agitation for change, especially from the Chartist movement. This was a mass working-class campaign, with some radical middle-class participation, stemming from disillusionment with the Reform Act and fuelled by the economic hardships of the 'hungry forties'. The 'People's Charter' demanded universal manhood suffrage by secret ballot, the abolition of the property qualification for candidates, the payment of MPs, annual parliaments, and the provision of equal electoral districts, so that constituencies should have approximately the same population. The fulfilment of these aims would certainly have made Britain into a democracy, but in 1848, the year of revolutions in Europe, the Chartists contented themselves with delivering a petition to Westminster, which the politicians ignored. The movement then faded away.

It seemed, for a time, that the Great Reform Act might be the permanent settlement which the Whigs had intended. Nevertheless, further reform legislation was passed, and Britain became more and more democratic. As the Chartists had recognised, democracy depended on a combination of factors – not only (i) on how many people had the vote, though this was obviously very important, but (ii) on whether the hustings could be freed from corruption and intimidation, (iii) on whether the electorate's choice might be extended by ending restrictions on who could become MPs, and (iv) on whether the distribution of seats reflected population density in the country. The growth of democracy after 1832 was a long and gradual process whose success cannot be assigned to just one factor. At least three forces were involved: popular and radical demands, changing political philosophies, and the self-interest and political manoeuvrings of the politicians at Westminster. Generally, all three factors were at work, in varying proportions, in producing legislative change. For the next major reform, historians tend to stress the third element, political expediency and self-interest, since, against expectations, legislation was brought about not by a Liberal but by a Conservative government.

1 The Second Reform Act, 1867

> **KEY ISSUES** Why did the Conservatives introduce a reform bill in 1866 and why did the Second Reform Act take the form that it did?

a) Revival of Reform

Enthusiasm for reform grew in the 1860s for a variety of reasons. British interests in foreign affairs – particularly in the movement for Italian unification and in the American Civil War, both of which were interpreted as popular struggles for freedom – increased demands for change at home. The death of Lord Palmerston, the Prime Minister, in 1865 also helped the cause: Palmerston's assertive foreign policy had been immensely popular, giving him the prestige to block efforts at parliamentary reform, the thought of which he detested. He once commented, caustically, that democracy would 'bring the scum to the top'. Now a new generation of politicians, with more flexible attitudes, became dominant. Furthermore, in 1866 an economic downturn increased social discontent, adding fuel to the calls for reform and boosting the membership of two recently-formed organisations, the Reform Union and the Reform League.

The Reform Union, founded in 1864, was Liberal, predominantly middle-class and led by wealthy Manchester merchants, manufacturers and radical MPs. Establishing branches throughout the country, and especially in the industrial towns, it aimed to produce political co-operation between the middle and working classes. Its demands included an extension of the franchise, secret voting and an even distribution of seats. The Reform League, founded the following year, was predominantly working-class and appreciably more radical, being supported by various left-wing organisations, including Karl Marx's 'First International'. The Union had more money, the League more members. In 1866 they worked together, both contributing to the growth of popular pressure for parliamentary reform.

b) Gladstone and the Liberal Reform Bill

After Palmerston's death Earl Russell (formerly Lord John Russell, who had introduced the 1831 Bill) became Prime Minister, but he was old and fuddled. The leading figure in the government was William Ewart Gladstone, the Chancellor of the Exchequer, a convert from the Tory party. He had visited Lancashire at the time of the 'cotton famine' (caused by the severing of cotton supplies to Britain during the American Civil War) and had been favourably impressed by working-class qualities. Encouraged by the veteran radical John Bright, he presented himself, and was accepted, as a popular politician – the 'People's William' – and became convinced that large numbers of working-class men could be trusted to exercise the franchise responsibly. In May 1864 he had told parliament that

i   every man who is not presumably incapacitated by some consideration of personal unfitness or of political danger, is morally entitled to come within the pale of the constitution. Of course, in giving utterance to such a proposition, I do not recede from the protest I have previously
5   made against sudden, or violent, or excessive or intoxicating change ... Hearts should be bound together by a reasonable extension, at fitting times and among selected portions of the people, of every benefit and every privilege that can be justly conferred upon them.

It was the first sentence of this statement, suggesting that almost every man had the right to vote, which caught the headlines, rather than his subsequent qualifications.

When Gladstone introduced a parliamentary bill in 1866, it became clear that he favoured only cautious reform. He would give the vote to respectable artisans but exclude the unskilled as well as the 'residuum' (the poor, irresponsible, shiftless and criminal). Gladstone and other Liberals had done their electoral homework: study of poll books revealed that the majority of working-class men who already had the vote cast it in favour of the Liberals, and it was therefore assumed that workers of a similar type – skilled and

WILLIAM EWART GLADSTONE (1809–98)

-Profile-

Gladstone had an exceptionally long and varied political career and was four times prime minister. The son of a rich Scottish Tory Liverpool merchant, he received an English aristocratic education at Eton and Christ Church, Oxford, and became a Tory MP in 1832, initially opposed to reform. A complex and contradictory person, both arrogant and humble, he was a devout high church Anglican always very concerned with religion and the Church, and he also gave much time and money to attempts to rescue prostitutes. Yet he was also a self-justifying political opportunist who advanced his own career and policies. His opponents, especially Disraeli, believed him a hypocrite. The Liberal MP Henry Labouchere famously remarked that he did not object to Gladstone having the ace of trumps up his sleeve, only to his pretence that God had put it there. Intelligent, hard-working and capable, Gladstone was an outstanding orator, parliamentarian and minister.

A devoted follower of Sir Robert Peel, Gladstone was President of the Board of Trade in 1843–6. When the Conservative party split over the corn laws, he was one of the Peelite minority. In the 1850s he joined the Whigs and was twice Chancellor of the Exchequer in that decade. Following the resignation of Lord Russell in 1866, Gladstone was leader of the Liberal party. He was essentially – except arguably on Ireland – a moderate reformer, but the reality was concealed by his reputation for moral rectitude and political progress. His first ministry was his greatest and saw Forster's Education Act (1870) and the Ballot Act (1872). His second ministry was dogged by misfortune but did see the Third Reform Act (1884–5). His third and fourth ministries were dominated by his unsuccessful Irish home rule bills.

'respectable' – would follow suit. His bill sought to enfranchise occupiers of property in the boroughs worth £7 in rent a year, as against the existing £10 qualification, and also those lodgers who rented property worth £10 a year – measures which, while increasing the number of working-class voters, would still have left them a minority of the total electorate. Probably about one in four men would have been able to vote, instead of the existing one in five.

Presenting the bill to the Commons, Gladstone insisted that

1 The £7 franchise will certainly work in a different manner ... The wages
   of a man occupying such a house would be a little under 26s [£1.30] a
   week. That sum is undoubtedly unattainable by the peasantry, and by
   mere hand labour, except in very rare circumstances, but it is generally
5 attainable by artisans and skilled labourers ... To give the vote to £6
   householders ... would be to transfer the balance of political power in
   the boroughs to the working classes ... We cannot consent to look
   upon this addition – considerable though it may be – of the working
   classes, as if it were an addition fraught with nothing but danger; we
10 cannot look upon it as a Trojan Horse ... filled with armed men bent
   on ruin, plunder and conflagration ... We believe that these persons
   whom we ask you to enfranchise ought rather to be welcomed as if
   they were recruits to your army.

The Reform League thought the measure far too limited, and radicals
like John Bright also considered that it did not go far enough, though
they pledged their support. However, right-wing Liberals and Whigs
(the aristocratic wing of the Liberal Party) decided that it would
enfranchise too many men from the working classes. Bright spoke of
their 'political Cave of Adullam' (a biblical reference to the cave
where 'every one that was discontented' gathered), and they became
known as the 'Adullamites'. Their most effective spokesman was
Robert Lowe, a barrister and former minister as well as a truculent
and myopic figure, who had been disgusted by the corruption and
vulgarity of popular politics in Australia. He claimed that the new
working-class voters would be corrupt and lacking in moral worth and
that therefore the bill would result in democracy and the end of the
existing social and political system. He asked the Commons in March
1866:

1 Is it not certain that in a few years from this the working men will be in
   a majority? Is it not certain that causes are at work which will have a
   tendency to multiply the franchise – that the £6 houses will become £7
   ones, and that £9 houses will expand to £10? There is no doubt an
5 immense power of expansion; and therefore ... it is certain that sooner
   or later we shall see the working classes in majority in the constituencies. Look at what that implies ... If you want venality, if you want
   ignorance, if you want drunkenness, and facility for being intimidated; or
   if, on the other hand, you want impulsive, unreflecting, and violent
10 people, where do you look for them in the constituencies? ... We know
   what those people are who live in small houses ... The first stage, I have
   no doubt will be an increase of corruption, intimidation, and disorder
   ... The second will be that the working men of England, finding themselves in a full majority of the whole constituency, will awake to a full
15 sense of their power.

Gladstone replied that Lowe and other critics misrepresented not only the bill but the working men whom it would enfranchise. But in fact Gladstone handled the Adullamites badly. With tact, he might have conciliated some of them, but instead his intransigence alienated them all. The result was a golden opportunity for the Tories: they co-operated with the Adullamites to defeat the bill in June, whereupon the Liberal government resigned.

c) The Conservatives' Reform Bill

Conservative leader Lord Derby formed an administration, with Benjamin Disraeli as Chancellor of the Exchequer. But it was a minority administration and so could pass legislation only if it gained sufficient support from opposition MPs. A Conservative government was in fact something of a rarity. The party had done badly since the 1832 Reform Act, and its days in office in 1866 seemed likely to be few. In these circumstances, Disraeli decided on a policy of boldness. Despite the traditional hostility of the party to parliamentary reform, he introduced his own reform bill. He reasoned that if the Conservatives could pilot such a measure through the Commons, they might gain politically: those newly enfranchised in the boroughs might well vote Conservative out of gratitude, while a Conservative bill could take all necessary precautions to preserve aristocratic power in the counties. Disraeli knew it would not be easy to secure the passage of reform legislation: his own backbenchers would not be keen, and in addition it could be passed only if a substantial minority of Liberals were won over. But if he could succeed where his detested rival Gladstone (who had now taken over as Liberal leader) had just failed, and in the process divide the Liberals, he would achieve a tremendous political victory. He was undoubtedly playing for high stakes. Failure might harm his career, but success would guarantee him the leadership of the party when Derby resigned.

Disraeli had another important motive. He claimed that he intended not only to 'extinguish Gladstone & Co.' but to 'destroy the present agitation'. A popular campaign pressing politicians for reform had recently begun. Bright and other radicals, together with the Reform League and the Reform Union, were holding a series of national meetings and demonstrations in favour of parliamentary reform. The most menacing incident occurred on 23 July 1866 when a demonstration organised in London by the Reform League got out of hand. What had been intended as a peaceful protest degenerated into violence in Hyde Park when an unruly mob joined in and the park railings were torn up. Skirmishes with the police continued for two days and troops had to be called out. An eyewitness judged that the police belabouring the front ranks of the crowd with their truncheons had little effect: 'Mrs Partington (see page 41) confronting the Atlantic with her broom was not a more ludicrous picture'. The country was certainly not on the verge of a violent revolution: indeed

BENJAMIN DISRAELI (1804–81)

-*Profile*-

The most colourful and unusual, and among the most controversial, of leading British politicians, Disraeli was twice prime minister. He was born in London of Italian Jewish descent, the son of a respectable Jewish writer of private means. Disraeli was educated at minor schools and in 1817 became a member of the Church of England, though continuing to be proud of his Jewishness. As a young man he was ambitious, romantic and financially and sexually disreputable. He wrote romantic novels of fashionable aristocratic life and managed, through his mistress, to procure election as a Conservative MP in 1837.

Disraeli was a flashy but unimportant backbencher, indeed an outsider in the party, and would probably have remained so but for the 1846 Corn Law crisis. His brilliant attacks on Peel for betraying the Conservative party over Corn Law repeal launched him into political prominence, and he became one of the leaders of the Conservative party, when they were usually out of office. His reform bill of 1867 was a brilliant gamble, and following Derby's resignation he was briefly prime minister in 1868. He was prime minister again in 1874–80, passing reforms which have been described by Paul Smith as 'a corpus of social legislation unparalleled until the ministries of 1905 and 1945'. He contributed much to making the Conservatives an electable party of government, identifying them with social reform, patriotism, the monarchy and imperialism.

some election riots in this period were far more menacing. Nevertheless, popular pressure was certainly a factor in the passage of reform legislation. It convinced many MPs that the reform issue had to be settled. To Disraeli, it provided an additional motive to press ahead.

Despite the resignation of three cabinet colleagues in protest, Disraeli introduced his bill in March 1867. It was a more moderate package of proposals than Gladstone's, one which the bulk of Tory backbenchers and the Adullamites might well accept. The borough franchise would be reserved for those who personally paid rates, thus excluding those householders ('compounders') whose rates were included in the rent they paid to landlords. In addition, university graduates, members of the learned professions and those with £50 savings were to have extra votes. Bright cast scorn on such 'fancy franchises', but many Conservatives viewed them favourably as providing sensible safeguards against the growth of a mass electorate – quantity would be balanced by 'quality'.

Gladstone attacked the measure with his usual fervour, but on this occasion his parliamentary barbs missed their target: his opponent simply would not stay still long enough to be hit. A sustained duel took place between Gladstone and Disraeli, and parliament witnessed a series of extraordinarily complex political manoeuvres. The result was that Disraeli's bill was changed out of all recognition and became far more radical than originally intended. Yet this must be seen as a great victory, not a defeat, for Disraeli, since in the course of debate he began to see the advantages of sponsoring a more thoroughgoing bill. In many ways he was being illogical: after all, the Conservatives had just thrown the Liberal government out of office, insisting that its proposals – which were more moderate than those now favoured by the Conservatives – were too extreme. But Disraeli was not concerned with consistency: he was after political success, and he sensed blood – Gladstone's. While regularly accepting radical amendments, he rejected all those of his Liberal enemy.

Commentators have praised Disraeli's brilliant opportunistic tactics and, above all, his flexibility. Having formed a temporary alliance with the right-wing (Adullamite) Liberals in 1866, to unseat the Liberal government, he now made common cause with the left-wing, radical element of the Party. He was willing to see borough representation radically reformed rather than allow the bill to be lost. Unlike Lowe, he did not fear the urban masses, and he was willing to accept a much larger working-class borough electorate. The 'fancy franchises' were abandoned and, in its final form, his bill would confer the vote on all male householders in the boroughs, regardless of the size or value of their house or of whether they were 'compounders' or paid rates in person. Debate centred on these eye-catching reforms, thereby obscuring the fact that voting in the counties, those bastions of Conservative support, would only be minimally changed. It also distracted attention from the area which Bright and others considered even more important than the franchise, the distribution of seats. The legislation would bring about only a small-scale redistribution, to the advantage of the Conservatives in that several county seats shed their urban areas and so became more certain than before to return Conservative candidates.

Disraeli played his cards with consummate skill. His was an outstanding parliamentary achievement. He judged correctly that the hunger of his backbenchers for office would overcome their scruples about extending the vote, and he consistently outmanoeuvred Gladstone, whose grip on the Liberal party was whereby weakened. Enough radical votes were won to enable the legislation to be passed.

'The Derby, 1867. Dizzy wins with "Reform Bill".' *Punch*, 25 May 1867.

Disraeli was thus the victor in the 1867 'Derby' (see the cartoon above). The Conservative Bill reached its final form in August 1867 and then became an Act. But the Conservatives were undoubtedly gambling. No one could be certain what effect the newly enfranchised would have on British politics. Disraeli hoped that, although the skilled workers were tied to the Liberal Party, the less skilled would vote Conservative. It has even been said that he discerned the working-class Conservative voter 'as a sculptor discerns the angel in a block of marble'. But Lord Derby called the Act 'a leap in the dark', while another observer compared it to 'shooting Niagara'.

d) The Causes of the Second Reform Act

The form taken by the Act undoubtedly owed much to Disraeli's parliamentary opportunism: in the course of debate he saw his chance to enhance the Conservative party at Westminster and boost his own career. Historians have devoted a tremendous amount of effort to charting exactly how he did it. However, political manoeuvring at Westminster should not monopolise our attention, and we must take due account of other factors, including reform agitation in general and the Hyde Park riots of 1866 in particular. Yet probably more important than working-class violence, which led to political anxiety, was working-class respectability, which assuaged political fears. There was far less agitation for reform in the 1860s than there had been in the 1830s and 1840s: certainly, popular pressure for reform in 1866 was on a far smaller scale than in 1832. It is significant that the riots in Hyde Park were put down with the help of a Reform League anxious to dissociate itself from mob violence. Karl Marx, while bemoaning the fact that the rioters had been so orderly, knew that the time was not right for revolution. Despite the slump in this year, economic conditions were in fact much better than they had been in the 1840s – some historians claim that there was a 'Mid-Victorian Boom' between 1850 and 1870 – and many members of the working classes, especially skilled workers, were becoming relatively affluent. Such men maintained ideals of sobriety, hard work, thrift and 'self-help' – values of which the middle classes heartily approved – and so they posed little threat to the governing elite, which decided it would not be taking too great a risk in entrusting them with the vote.

Nor should we allow Disraeli's brilliant, and somewhat cynical, political coup to detract attention from changes in political principle. Political assumptions about the franchise had shifted since the debates on the Great Reform Bill. Admittedly most MPs continued to deny that they were democrats, but, even so, they had undoubtedly moved closer to democracy. No longer did parliamentary debaters insist that the franchise should be determined solely by wealth or property. Political philosophers like John Stuart Mill, who was an MP at this time, advocated that all 'responsible' or 'full' citizens should be enfranchised – in other words those educated sufficiently to exercise the vote prudently. Therefore the debate centred not so much on whether it was wise, in the abstract, to extend the franchise but on the likely political effects of giving the vote to certain categories of people. Indeed it was implicit in many speeches that, although the franchise was a privilege rather than an automatic right, almost everyone might be given the vote eventually. No one could claim the vote on principle, but then again virtually no one would remain forever ineligible on principle. Such ideas created the political climate that made it possible for the Second Reform Bill to be passed.

e) The Second Reform Act

The Second Reform Act was silent on issues like the secret ballot and payment for MPs, and parliament rejected the idea, put forward by John Stuart Mill, that women should have the vote on the same terms as men. But the new legislation extended the franchise and redistributed seats in England and Wales:

Franchise

In the boroughs
(i) all male householders could vote, regardless of the type of dwelling they occupied, providing they had been in occupancy for 12 months,
(ii) lodgers occupying premises worth at least £10 per annum in rent could also vote, again providing they had been resident for 12 months.

In the counties
(i) arrangements were left as in 1832 (i.e. 40-shilling freeholders), but in addition
(ii) owners or leaseholders of lands of yearly value of £5 or more could vote, together with owners of lands to a rateable value of £12 a year, who also paid poor rates.

Redistribution
(i) 45 seats were taken from boroughs with under 10,000 inhabitants and 7 towns were disfranchised for corruption.
(ii) 25 seats were given to counties, 20 seats were created for new boroughs, 6 boroughs received 1 extra seat each, and London University was given a seat.

Similar Acts were passed for Scotland and Ireland in 1868.

f) Results of the Second Reform Act

The most obvious result of the 1867 Act was that the electorate was significantly enlarged. Approximately 1,120,000 new voters were added to the previous total of about 1,400,000. About one in three adult men could vote, instead of one in five. We cannot be sure of exact figures, however, since the provisions of the Act were in some ways ambiguous: in particular the definition of a 'household' was interpreted differently by the local authorities, many of which went to great pains to prevent 'feckless slum-dwellers' from qualifying for the vote. The greatest increase was in the boroughs, where the total number of voters rose by 135 per cent, and in some industrial cities the figures were much higher. For example, Birmingham's electorate rose from 8,000 to 43,000. As a result, the boroughs henceforth had a predominantly working-class electorate. However, the increase in the counties was only 45 per cent, so that county constituencies remained middle-class and many continued to be dominated by aristocratic patrons.

For the first time in British history, the overall electorate contained a majority of working-class voters, but the impact of this was minimised by the conservative nature of the Act's redistribution. The distribution of constituencies still did not correspond to that of population. Rural areas were still over-represented relative to industrial, and the south and west of England relative to the rest of the country. Whereas the south-west of England had 45 MPs, for instance, the north-east, despite a population three times as large, had only 32. There were still enormous discrepancies in the population of constituencies.

The effects of the Act on party politics are not easy to quantify. There were gains and losses for both parties in electoral terms. Although the Liberals won the 1868 general election, in the longer term the Conservatives probably gained most, in 1874 winning their first clear majority in the Commons since 1841 and scoring a narrow margin of total election victories between the Second (1867) and the Third (1884) Reform Acts. The Act led to improvements in organisation for both parties. The increased electorate, especially in the boroughs, engendered more efficient party machines to capture the new voters. The National Union of Conservative Associations was formed in 1867 and the National Liberal Federation in 1877.

Finally, the 1867 Act contributed to the introduction of the 1870 Education Act, which recognised education as a public service. Politicians believed it was necessary to 'educate our new masters'. But mass education would affect voter and non-voter alike, and so made a further enlargement of the electorate likely at a later date.

2 The Removal of Intimidation and Corruption

> **KEY ISSUES** For what reasons, and with what effect, was legislation passed against corruption and intimidation at elections?

a) The Ballot Act, 1872

i) Background and Causes

Radicals had been calling for a secret ballot since the 1770s. An attempt had been made to include such a provision in the 1831 Reform Bill, and it had figured among Chartist demands. Reformers believed that a truly representative system was impossible under the old arrangement of public voting and that only a secret ballot could ensure voters' freedom of choice by preventing corruption and by protecting them from intimidation. They also believed that it would be in their own political interests, reasoning that many more votes would be cast for radical candidates if only electors were freed from undue pressure. On the other hand, most peers and many politicians insisted that a secret ballot would be 'un-English'. They argued there was something cowardly and furtive about voting that was not open and public. In addition, they were unsure what the results of a secret ballot would be and feared the worst. Conservative cabinets certainly opposed such a reform, while the Liberals tended to be divided on the issue.

In Gladstone's first ministry (1868–74) a secret ballot was conceded. There were two reasons for this. One was the advocacy of the veteran radical John Bright. He had been calling for this measure ever since the 1830s; now the politicians listened. Gladstone wished to increase radical support for his new government by including Bright within his cabinet, but the price of his participation was the introduction of secret ballot legislation. Gladstone personally disliked the proposal but was willing to acquiesce. Yet a ballot bill might well have foundered in parliament had it not been for the second reason, revelations about the conduct of the 1868 general election.

In 1868, as in previous elections, there had been corruption, intimidation and violence. What was unusual was the publicity this election achieved, both in the press and the law courts (where disputed results were decided). At Blackburn, for instance, a journalist described an election riot as a result of which 'the sickening sight of men with blood flowing from their heads and faces met one at every turn.' The government then initiated a committee of enquiry, with Bright among its members. It reported in 1870, stating that

1 With regard to Parliamentary Elections in Boroughs your Committee have examined many witnesses, but the evidence does no more than confirm what has been frequently established before ... In former and in the last Elections various corrupt practices, of which bribery and
5 treating were the chief, have prevailed, and to such an extent as to invalidate many Elections ... It has been proved that in some instances rioting and violence to persons and property have occurred ... so as to interfere with the freedom of the Election, while in a much larger class of case Elections are accompanied by drunkenness and disorder ...
10 County Elections ... have been in the main free from bribery. It is, however, alleged that intimidation and undue influence are very largely practised in county elections, and evidence from Wales and Scotland, to the effect that tenants have been actually turned out of their farms on account of their votes, has been brought before us ... It is certain ...
15 that an influence, exceeding in a greater or less degree the legitimate influence which a popular and respected landlord must always exercise in his neighbourhood, is often brought to bear on tenant farmers, and other voters in agricultural districts.

The report favoured the introduction of secret voting.

ii) The Ballot Act of 1872

The government's first ballot bill was rejected by parliament in 1871. In 1872 another, similar bill passed the Commons but was criticised in the Lords. The veteran philanthropist and social reformer Lord Shaftesbury objected that the bill would 'force a man to slink away like a creeping animal' instead of discharge his duty in the face of his fellow-citizens. Earl Russell insisted that a secret ballot would increase corruption, including bribery and the impersonation of electors. Yet theirs were minority viewpoints and the Ballot Act was passed in 1872. Henceforth electors were to vote by secretly marking a printed ballot paper with a cross and placing it in a sealed ballot box. If an elector was illiterate or blind, the election official was to mark the paper for him. Votes were then counted in the presence of the candidates' agents.

iii) Results
The first by-election under the new rules was held in 1872 – when a correspondent of *The Times* was favourably impressed with the sobriety and order of the voters – and the first general election in 1874. No one could be sure what effect the Act would have. Like the reform acts, it was 'a leap in the dark', and similarly its results were less than had been hoped or feared. It certainly did not eliminate corruption overnight, and its effect on rural constituencies was limited: doubts about how secret the ballot actually was, together with continued deference, meant that landlord influence continued to be important in many areas until the First World War. As late as 1910 a Liberal candidate complained that 'One of the greatest difficulties has been to convince some of the timid rural voters of the absolute secrecy of the ballot'. Nor did the secret ballot immediately diminish the influence of some factory-owners over their employees in the urban constituencies.

Nevertheless, in the longer term, the Ballot Act undoubtedly had a major effect on British politics by reducing the pressure landlords or employers could exert. It facilitated the political growth of groups, like the Home Rulers in Ireland, opposing the traditionally powerful figures of particular areas. Overall, by enabling electors to vote as they chose rather than as others commanded, it made the electoral system more representative and democratic. (Perhaps its only drawback was that, by abolishing poll books, it made the electoral historian's job that much harder!)

b) The Corrupt and Illegal Practices Prevention Act, 1883
i) Continued Corruption
The increased size of the electorate, together with the secret ballot, meant that intimidation could rarely decide an election result. But this should not lead us to suppose that candidates relied solely on political argument to win over the voters. Instead they increased their expenditure on 'colourable employment' (the temporary, but unnecessary, employment of local people in order to gain their votes and those of their families) and on the purchase of local goods. A Conservative politician wrote of an electoral contest that

ı The practice had become almost universal for candidates to lavish immense sums of money upon purposes not in themselves corrupt, but quite useless for the attainment of any legitimate object. The true aim

of such expenditure was to distribute money amongst the greatest
5 possible number of electors, and a candidate who refused to conform
to this universal custom had, or was believed to have, no chance of
being returned ... Every article purchased, every service rendered, was
paid for at more than double its market value ... Both sides concurred
in a complete distrust of the post-office, and employed an army of mes-
10 sengers to deliver their communications to the electors ... The ingenuity of the election managers was taxed to invent the greatest possible
amount of clerical work in the few real committee-rooms, and twice as
many clerks were engaged as were necessary to perform it.

Another politician wrote of his election in 1880:

1 It is noteworthy that our chief expense was due to our agents having,
according to the custom of the day, engaged every conveyance in the
division for the day of the poll, in order to ensure reaching the limited
number of polling-places, and the creation of a corresponding difficulty
5 for our opponents.

ii) The Corrupt and Illegal Practices Act

Politicians disliked heavy election costs, especially since the secret
ballot meant that those who accepted inducements would not necessarily do the honourable thing and vote for their benefactor: some
electors might even take bribes from both candidates. In addition,
radicals had long been urging successive governments to introduce
legislation to eliminate corruption. Gladstone's second government
therefore decided to act. The Liberals were the more likely party to
grasp the nettle of corruption: after all, the Conservatives tended to
be wealthier, and therefore the reduction of expenditure might well
harm their electoral performance the most. On the other hand,
Conservative pockets would benefit, and, as it turned out, the
Conservative leaders decided to support the Liberals in their attempt
to reduce corruption. Hence the bill passed.

The Act fixed maximum legal election expenses and numbers of
paid employers (clerks and messengers) per candidate, levels varying
with the type of constituency and size of electorate, and – to the
protest of cabbies – forbade the hiring of vehicles to carry voters. Its
penalties were much more stringent than those of previous legislation. It laid down that electoral corruption was to be punished by
fines and imprisonment and, if the guilty candidate had won the election, by forfeiture of the seat.

iii) Results

The 1883 Act has been described as 'a landmark in the struggle for
electoral purity ... its effect was to transform the whole character of
British electioneering within a generation'. Certainly it had important
consequences and greatly reduced corruption. In the next general
election, held in 1885, total official expenditure fell by three-quarters.

The average cost per vote in the United Kingdom fell, according to official figures, from 18s 9d in 1880 to 3s 8d in 1910 (i.e. 97.75p to 18.3p). Candidates and their agents tried to keep within the terms of the Act, if only because their opponents ('poachers turned game-keepers') could use their infringements against them.

By limiting expenses and paid employees, the Act put the onus on politicians to recruit unpaid volunteers, with a consequent stimulation to local party organisation. But even so, the Act had its limitations, and politics continued to be expensive. The law only applied to elections, so that between elections a rich MP or prospective candidate could 'nurse' a constituency by lavish expenditure. Furthermore, the banning of hired transport benefited some candidates more than others: it particularly helped those with richer supporters, who would usually have their own means of transportation.

c) The Reduction of Violence

There were no specific laws aimed at eliminating rowdiness or violent intimidation, despite the fact that between 1865 and 1885 there were at least 71 incidents of serious disorder. Nevertheless, from the 1860s there was an unmistakable decline of physical intimidation and violence at elections. This can be attributed to a number of factors, including the indirect consequences of legislation. By abolishing the traditional public nomination of candidates, the Corrupt and Illegal Practices Act decreased election 'treating' and so minimised the drunkenness which in the past had characterised elections and had often led to riots. Such legislation also made candidates and their agents discourage violence lest it result in loss of the seat on petition. In 1911 the Hartlepool Liberal MP was unseated because his agent had hired a band of miners for 'demonstrations', thereby creating an atmosphere of intimidation in the constituency. More effective policing was also a major factor in the general reduction of violence in British politics.

d) Conclusion

Electoral violence and corruption lingered on into the early-twentieth century. Yet they had ceased to be a significant part of the electoral system and had instead become minimal and anachronistic survivals. The 1883 Corrupt and Illegal Practices Act, together with the 1872 Ballot Act, undoubtedly did much to reduce corruption, and consequent violence, at elections, but they alone do not explain its decline. They must be seen within a wider context. The disenfranchisement of small corrupt boroughs was also vitally important, as was the increased size of the electorate in the country as a whole. Constituencies had become too large for bribery to be worthwhile, while British society as a whole was becoming less brutal and violent.

Also important was the growth of a new set of political attitudes, stemming from the 'nonconformist conscience' and from radical demands for electoral 'purity' which stressed the need for higher standards; and while many politicians sincerely believed in this new political culture, others swam with the tide and conformed from expediency.

What cannot be doubted is that the reduction, and in time the virtual elimination, of electoral intimidation and corruption was a vitally important part of the democratisation of the British parliamentary system. It complemented the extension of the franchise: not only could more people vote, but they could vote freely for the candidates of their choice.

3 The Third Reform Act, 1884–5

> **KEY ISSUE** Why did both parties agree on a further reform act in 1884?

The Third Reform Act was the least dramatic of the nineteenth-century reform acts. It was occasioned by no deaths, no burning of houses and no revolutionary threat. Instead its passage was marked merely by speeches, a few minor riots and a secret deal between ageing political leaders, neither of whom really wanted electoral reform. Nevertheless, the Third Reform Act was important and gave the vote to a larger number of men than its more dramatic predecessors.

a) Background

The First and Second Reform Acts had shifted ruling-class political attitudes in Britain. After 1867 most politicians of all parties, whether they wanted it or not, accepted that further extensions of the franchise were inevitable sooner or later. The important thing, therefore, was for each party to ensure that reform was in its own interests – that whatever legislation was passed enfranchised more of its own supporters than likely opposition voters.

The 1867 Act had left the majority of men, and all women, without the vote. The largest category of unenfranchised men lived in the counties. The franchise was far more restricted there than in the boroughs, and it was this anomaly which helped to bring about further reform. The main impetus for change within government came from the radicals, and especially from the former Mayor of Birmingham (see page 97), the ambitious and dynamic Joseph Chamberlain, President of the Board of Trade in Gladstone's second ministry. He was disliked by the Prime Minister, an emotion he reciprocated, but Chamberlain had his own plans for the political future. He and fellow radicals wanted to take control of the Liberal Party, exclude the old-fashioned and aristocratic Whigs, and win a general election on a platform of radical reforms. They assumed that Gladstone, an old man who had already once retired, could not continue long as party leader. Electoral reform was a crucial part of their strategy.

In the past radicals had accepted the restrictive county franchise because they assumed that rural workers were apathetic and deferential – that they would vote, if they bothered to do so at all, the way their employers or landlords dictated. However, the Ballot Act of 1872 made it possible for all men to vote freely, and there were soon unmistakable signs of untapped Liberal support in the counties, especially among coal-miners. Well-organised in trade unions, and aware that some of their fellow-miners in the boroughs already had the vote, the miners were beginning to throw their weight behind the Liberal Party. Northumberland and Durham miners campaigned for the Liberals in the 1874 election, and one of their leaders, Thomas Burt, was elected an MP. But they made it clear that their continued adherence depended upon an extension of the franchise. Their cause was taken up by Chamberlain, who believed that an increase in Liberal – and moreover radical – votes in the counties could further his aim of transforming the party.

In 1883 the radicals held meetings to arouse popular support for electoral reform. Nevertheless there was far less public clamour for change than in 1832 or even in 1866. The initiative remained firmly with the politicians. Gladstone, the Prime Minister, was reluctant to accept reform, being far more concerned to settle the problems of Ireland, an issue with which some believed him positively obsessed. But when his ministry began to lurch from crisis to crisis, with disappointingly few achievements, he was persuaded, in the end, to agree to moderate parliamentary reform. By this means he might retain radical support and regain popularity in the country.

b) The Reform Bill: Crisis and Compromise

In 1884 a Liberal reform bill, extending the franchise in the counties, was accepted by the Commons and was then debated by the House of Lords, where the Conservatives led by Lord Salisbury had a majority. Salisbury was a rich, landowning aristocrat who was profoundly conservative and politically pessimistic. Loathing radicalism and democracy, he had resigned from the cabinet in 1867 in protest at Disraeli's reform bill. His most consistent political aim was to preserve the aristocracy and the Church of England for as long as possible, and he had no faith in the emergence of working-class Conservative voters. But he was no unthinking reactionary, and indeed his successful outmanoeuvring of rivals for the leadership of the Conservative Party after the death of Disraeli in 1881 had shown him to be a remarkably astute and skilful politician. While having conservative long-term aims, he was quite prepared to foster short-term changes, and in 1884 he saw that electoral reform need not be a disaster for his party. Like most Conservatives, he expected to lose politically from an expansion of the county franchise, since the newly-enfranchised were likely to vote Liberal. But if seats could be redistributed in a way that would favour the Conservatives, his party would not be swamped by Liberal majorities.

Radicals like Chamberlain welcomed confrontation. They wanted to use the conflict to rouse the country against the Lords and to fight a general election on the issue of 'The Peers against the People', insisting that the powers of the Upper House should be 'mended' (i.e. reduced) or 'ended' altogether. In London a Democratic Committee for the Abolition of the House of Lords was established. Yet the response in the country was not as great as the radicals had hoped. There were some riots, but relatively few, and they were feeble in comparison with those that had occurred in 1832 or 1866. As for Gladstone, he was not at all impressed with the radicals' campaign. Nor were the Whigs. The last thing they wanted was the political mobilisation of the masses. They certainly did not wish to abolish the aristocracy or the House of Lords. Like Salisbury (and like Queen Victoria) they wanted compromise not confrontation and called for the problem to be solved by negotiations.

Meetings took place between Gladstone, Salisbury and other leading figures. These secret talks were in fact unprecedented, for never before had rival party leaders discussed the details of a measure to be introduced into parliament. Salisbury, who was in a strong negotiating position because of the Lords' veto, was mainly concerned with redistribution, a sphere in which he wished to see changes so major that Gladstone was shocked by his lack of respect for tradition. But the Conservative leader knew that there had been a massive growth of towns and cities, and of their suburbs, many of which contained only working-class or only middle-class residents, and to his mind this single-class residential segregation held the key to his party's survival. He therefore called for the ending of a system of (mostly) double-member constituencies – which would probably elect fewer Conservatives as the vote was extended to more and more men – and its replacement by smaller, single-member constituencies. Under this arrangement, there would be a substantial number of middle-class constituencies which could be relied upon to return Conservative candidates. Conservative minorities in old constituencies might even become majorities in new ones.

The party leaders negotiated a compromise agreement, the 'Arlington Street compact', by which the Liberals attained the franchise extension they wanted in return for the redistribution Salisbury was after. As a result, the political crisis ended and the Third Reform Act was passed.

c) The Third Reform Act

The term 'Third Reform Act' is not a strictly accurate one. In reality there were two separate pieces of legislation, the Franchise Act (1884) and the Redistribution Act (1885), both of which applied to the entire United Kingdom. Together they shaped the electoral system which lasted until 1918.

The Franchise Act gave the vote to male householders and £10 lodgers in the counties, providing they had occupied their houses or lodgings for twelve months. It also created the £10 occupation franchise, applying mainly to those who occupied shops or offices. In addition, the older franchises also applied. In short, the 1867 borough franchise was extended to the counties, so that the householder franchise became the main means by which men qualified for the vote in the United Kingdom. In 1911 84.3 per cent of the electorate was registered under it.

The Redistribution Act brought about the most thorough redistribution of seats in the whole of the century. A total of 160 seats were redistributed. In England and Wales 79 boroughs with under 15,000 inhabitants lost one seat each. London's constituencies increased from 22 to 55, while other cities and counties also gained MPs. The old county divisions were cut into single-member constituencies, and indeed most constituencies henceforth had only a single Member of Parliament: as a result, they were no longer historic communities but artificial units based approximately on numbers.

d) Results

The legislation added more voters than either of the earlier reform acts. It increased the number of those eligible to vote in the United Kingdom from 3 million to almost 6 million. Henceforth approximately two in three adult men could vote, instead of one in three. It also changed the nature of the county electorate, enfranchising many agricultural workers and miners. In addition, redistribution changed the system of constituencies to correspond more – though not entirely – with the distribution of population. Urban and industrial areas (such as Lancashire and the West Riding of Yorkshire) received more MPs, while county towns had fewer. The sub-division of city constituencies created safe Conservative seats, as Salisbury had intended, in the business areas and the suburbs (e.g. Leeds Central and Leeds North).

Both the main parties gained from the Third Reform Act in that the increased electorate stimulated them to improve the professionalism of their party machines; but on the whole they gained in different ways. The radical Liberals successfully appealed to the new rural voters in 1885, and the Liberals certainly won that year's general election. Yet the Conservatives did better than before in the boroughs.

The Act also strengthened the radicals in the Liberal Party: in the past, in two-member constituencies, a Whig had often been paired with a radical, whereas in the new single-member constituencies fewer Whigs were selected as candidates. In Ireland, the new dispensation favoured the Home Rulers at the expense of the Liberals.

The Third Reform Act also contributed to the growth of the 'Lib–Labism' – working-class support for the Liberals and the election of working-class ('Labour') MPs who, while part of the parliamentary Liberal Party, were independent on specifically working-class and trade union issues. Lib–Lab candidates benefited enormously from the fact that the Act created constituencies with working-class majorities, notably the coal-mining areas. Such MPs were usually salaried trade union leaders, whose unions would pay their political expenses. Two had been elected in 1874, but this number increased to 13 in 1885.

All the reform acts contributed to the decline in the political power and influence of the aristocracy, the Third more than its predecessors. By reducing the number of rural seats, and at the same time enlarging the county electorate, the Act ensured that landowners would have less influence than ever before. Electoral patronage survived in only a few constituencies, and even there the patrons' hold tended to be fragile rather than absolute. According to one historian, after 1885 there were only a dozen county constituencies in which influence was exercised by important patrons, a mere one-seventh of the number of seats dominated by patronage after the 1867 Act. The number of aristocratic ministers and MPs also declined, even though their numbers were still significant. Many members of the Commons argued that the sole source of political legitimacy lay in direct election by the people, an argument which threw their Lordships on to the defensive. In contrast, the act boosted the position of the middle classes. After the 1885 general election, manufacturers and commercial men outnumbered landowners for the first time in the history of the House of Commons. There was still a partnership in British politics between the middle classes and the aristocracy, but the former had become the dominant element.

4 The Electoral System, 1885–1918

KEY ISSUES Why were fresh reforms introduced in 1918? In particular, why did women receive the vote, though not on the same terms as men?

a) Democratic Deficiencies

The electoral system was far more representative than ever before after the reforms of 1884–5, but Britain was still not a democracy. All women were denied the vote in general elections and so was a substantial minority of men, including lodgers paying less than the specified rent, adult sons living with their parents, servants occupying their employers' houses, members of the armed forces, men of no fixed abode and all those in receipt of poor relief. Residence requirements also limited the electorate. Eligibility to vote depended on twelve months' residence in the constituency, and this ruled out many working-class men, who often moved about in search of work. Furthermore, registering for a vote was an extremely complicated and lengthy business. Instead of introducing a new, simple franchise, each reform act added new franchises to existing ones, with the result that many men were uncertain whether they were eligible or not. The result was that a large number of men – perhaps several millions – who were eligible to vote did not end up on the registers. One observer described this system as 'democracy tempered by registration'. In practice, a maximum of 60 per cent of adult males were able to vote in general elections after the Third Reform Act. On the other hand, some men qualified for several votes. 'Plural voting', as it was known, was not possible in the same constituency, but there was no legal maximum to the number of votes for which a man might qualify in different constituencies. Many middle-class men qualified for two votes, one as householders and another as owners of business premises, while graduates of Oxford, Cambridge and London Universities could vote for their university seat. Sir Charles Dilke had nine votes and Joseph Chamberlain six. Gladstone complained in 1879 that it was 'the rarest thing in the world' to meet a poor voter who had more than one vote or a 'gentleman' who had only one. By 1910 there were estimated to be about 500,000 plural voters. Partly as a result of this and partly because of the ineligibility of some men to vote, the middle classes, who comprised about 20 per cent of the adult male population, formed about 40 per cent of the electorate.

Clearly this system made it more difficult for Labour or socialist parties to emerge at Westminster: their 'natural' voters, the working classes, formed a large majority of the population but a much smaller majority of the electorate. The distribution of seats was also weighted against them. Despite the redistribution of 1885, some parts of the country were under-represented in parliament (including Scotland, the north of England and urban areas in general), while others (including Ireland, the south of England and rural areas) were over-represented. Furthermore, industrial constituencies tended to be among the largest in the country, thus limiting the number of potential working-class MPs. Working-class men also found it difficult to stand for election. Property qualifications for MPs had been abolished in 1858, but the costs of elections continued to be high despite the 1883 Corrupt and Illegal Practices Act. For instance, candidates would have to pay the expenses of the electoral returning officer, which might easily amount to several hundred pounds, and were expected to pay the salary of a constituency agent as well. In addition, MPs were unpaid. Britain could not be called a true democracy when the voters' choice was limited by a system weighted in favour of the rich and against the poor. Expense was one factor in the high incidence of uncontested elections in this period: between 1880 and 1910 there was an average of 136 unopposed returns at each general election, 20 per cent of the total number of seats. An important change occurred in 1911 when the Liberals introduced payment for MPs of £400 per annum, a substantial middle-class salary; but the system continued to be dominated by the wealthy.

The system was criticised by radicals, socialists and trade unionists. The Liberal Party also called for reform, demanding manhood suffrage in the 1890s and, while in office from 1905, introducing a series of bills against plural voting. However, the Conservatives opposed reform whilst they were in office and, during Liberal administrations, vetoed reform through their majority in the House of Lords (see pages 130–2).

b) Women's Suffrage

By far the greatest challenge to the electoral status quo after 1885 came from the women's suffrage movement. This was part of the wider attempt by women to improve their position in society. The extension of male suffrage made the non-enfranchisement of women seem still more unjust, since an illiterate man could vote but not a female graduate, and encouraged women to campaign for the vote. Similarly, the fact that some women could vote in local government elections (see page 103) made the prohibition of their participation in national contests seem anomalous.

The period after 1840 was one of immense, if gradual and patchy, changes in the opportunities, rights and roles of women. They resulted from a combination of interconnected factors – demographic, ideological, educational and economic. Together they provided the context for the women's suffrage movement. After the Second Reform Act the campaign for women's votes gained support from increasing numbers of women and some men. Sympathetic MPs attempted to introduce legislation giving women the vote, but the majority of each party was opposed to women's suffrage. Most men, including even John Bright, believed that nature had ordained 'separate spheres' for the sexes: while men were intellectual and so could take a constructive interest in politics, women were emotional and so should confine themselves to their roles as wives and mothers. (Ideally, unmarried – 'surplus' – women should not exist; but, failing this, they were to devote themselves to male relatives or emigrate.) To most leading politicians, 'votes for women' remained a peripheral issue; but it was hard for them to ignore the National Union of

Women's Suffrage Societies founded in 1897 by Mrs Millicent Fawcett and impossible to ignore the Women's Social and Political Union, founded by the dynamic and domineering Mrs Emmeline Pankhurst in 1903. Whereas Fawcett's 'suffragists' were moderate and law-abiding, Fawcett herself being married to the postmaster-general in Gladstone's second ministry, Pankhurst's 'suffragettes' were much more militant, holding demonstrations with bands and banners, partly in order to provide 'photo opportunities' for the popular press. In 1905 they disrupted the Liberals' election campaign, then in the following years escalated their tactics to include vandalism, arson and physical attacks on ministers. The militants won great publicity but their violence alienated many, and their contribution to winning votes for women has long been disputed. Probably it was the moderates who gained more support.

Women's suffrage cut across party divisions. The Conservative and Liberal Parties both contained supporters and opponents. The Liberals were in power after 1905, and whereas their leader, Herbert Asquith, was against extending the vote to women, most members of the party were broadly in favour; but they were convinced that women should not be enfranchised under the existing arrangements, since these would discriminate in favour of middle-class women and so probably benefit the Conservatives. In their view, women could only have the vote as part of a wider package which would include more working-class men. No such arrangements had been worked out by the time war broke out in August 1914.

c) The Fourth Reform Act, 1918

In February 1918 thousands of men were dying, horribly, on the Western Front, and the war seemed likely to continue for at least another year. As a result, the passage of the Representation of the People Act by Lloyd George's coalition government was relatively little noticed by the public. It was not the result of any great popular clamour: indeed even the suffragettes had decided to cease their campaigns for the duration of the war. More than any of its predecessors, therefore, the Fourth Reform Act came about as a result of the initiatives of the politicians.

The short-term origins of the Act go back to the problems of Asquith's government in 1915: an election was due shortly but the electoral registers were out of date and would have to be changed to take account of the men serving in the forces. The problem was referred to a special conference of peers and MPs presided over by the Speaker in 1916, and this recommended substantial changes, including universal manhood suffrage. Liberals and Labour had called for manhood suffrage before the war; the Conservatives had traditionally opposed such a measure but they now changed their position, partly in the hope that the newly enfranchised men might well vote for the Conservatives (generally depicted as the patriotic party) after their experience of military service. But it was an agreement to retain plural voting, which the other parties really wished to abolish, which finally won them over. Underlying parliament's initiative was the assumption that, although there was no overt demand for an extension of the franchise, the public undoubtedly expected reform. Any man who was prepared to fight and die for his country had surely earned the right to vote in its elections. Some believed that, after the war, the ex-serviceman might turn against the politicians who had failed to enfranchise them. Everything possible had to be done to prevent Bolshevism in Britain. Hence the Act gave the vote to all men aged 21 and over, as well as to those aged 19 and over who were on active service in the war.

i) Votes for Women

The Speaker's conference also recommended that women should be enfranchised, and parliament voted by large majorities that women aged 30, providing they or their husband were householders, should be allowed to vote. This was the most contentious part of the 1918 legislation. Why did parliament accept a measure which it had earlier rejected? Probably the answer lies partly in the fact that, even before the war, a majority of MPs had favoured some form of women's suffrage, so long as it was unlikely to be to the disadvantage of their own party; and now women's war work – as nurses, as munitions and agricultural workers, as well as in the auxiliary fighting services – seemed to have earned them the nation's gratitude. There may also have been a wish to prevent renewed suffragette violence after the war.

No one could be certain how many electors would be added to the registers, but the politicians judged correctly that men would still outnumber women. The electorate was increased by over 5 million men – producing around 13 million male voters – and 8 million women, so that the total electorate was trebled. The 1918 Act therefore gave the vote to more people than all the previous reform acts put together. As a result, Britain had become much more democratic than ever before, a process boosted by several other provisions of the Act. Plural votes were henceforth limited: an individual could exercise a maximum of two constituency votes (for residence and business premises or residence and university). There was also a redistribution of seats with the aim of creating uniform, single-member constituencies of about 70,000 inhabitants. Finally, elections were made much cheaper for candidates: no longer would they have to pay the expenses of the returning officer, who would now be reimbursed from public funds. This change was one factor in the rise of the Labour Party after the war.

5 Conclusion

> **KEY ISSUE** How significant were the series of reforms from 1867 to 1918?

Between 1832 and 1918 the British electoral system was transformed. Each electoral reform, by itself, may seem an undramatic change, no more than an evolutionary addition to the existing system; but the cumulative effect of the series of reforms passed during this period was surely revolutionary. By 1918 three-quarters of the adult population could vote, and vote freely, for a range of candidates. Once a breach had been made in the unreformed system in 1832, no electoral arrangements had remained fixed for very long. One reform led to another: the 1867 Reform Act for instance, which gave the vote to householders in the boroughs, led to demands for similar provisions in the counties, which were accepted in 1884. (Similarly, the 1918 legislation, with its unequal treatment of women, was unlikely to last long.) Disraeli was correct in his judgement of 1853 that once reform was begun 'you could not find any point to stop at short of the absolute sovereignty of the people'. By 1918 this sovereignty had indeed been recognised. It is very tempting, therefore, to judge that the Whig historians (see page 6) had been correct, and to see democratic progress in this period as a glorious process which was infinitely preferable to the violent upheavals seen elsewhere and which was also somehow 'natural' if not indeed 'inevitable'.

Perhaps the Whigs *were* correct. The development of democracy in Britain can indeed be seen as essentially a success story. But it should not be assumed that, by 1918, the electoral system had reached a state of perfection. Undoubtedly Britain had become more democratic; whether it had actually become a true democracy is examined in detail in chapter 8.

What of the process by which change came about? Was that a glorious chapter in Britain's history? Without doubt, reform was slow and intermittent between 1832 and 1918, and those who regard the unfolding of a democratic system as somehow 'inevitable' would do well to remember that some people struggled very hard to foster, and others to prevent, change. Perhaps, as one historian has remarked, 'nothing is inevitable until it happens'. Certainly other countries, while experiencing similar social and economic changes in the nineteenth century, developed very different political systems. The Whig interpretation therefore does less than justice to the complexity of the process by which Britain was democratised.

We have seen that electoral change arose from a background of socio-economic development which altered the demographic map of Britain and, specifically, from a series of separate legislative measures, each of which had its own particular, and often very complicated, causes. But it is possible to identify three overall factors of major importance: pressures, politicians and principles.

Pressures came from the mass of unenfranchised people, men and women, demanding the vote, and from the radicals who organised and spoke for them. The degree of force they could muster at particular junctures is a highly controversial issue. Admittedly it is difficult to generalise about the importance of pressures over the period 1815–1918 as a whole; but several things can be said with some confidence. First, that without mass pressure British political life would not have assumed the democratic shape that it did. It also seems likely that, as the nineteenth century proceeded, mass agitation for reform declined significantly, at least in the campaign for men's votes. Britain may have been on the verge of revolution in 1832 – the issue is hotly disputed – but few have argued that revolution was possible at any time thereafter, even during the suffragettes' campaigns before 1914. However, it should not be assumed that such influences ceased to be important. Rather, they changed their form. Perhaps victory in 1832 led to the conviction that reform could be achieved peacefully: certainly, as politics became more representative, people saw less and less need to riot on the streets. Pressures could be applied more subtly, through 'public opinion', as expressed through meetings, the ballot box and the media.

Public pressure is a factor that should never be ignored in any analysis of political reform. Yet the masses and the radicals did not decide the actual terms of the reform legislation. However strong the pressure from the reform movement, governments remained in control and made the detailed decisions. Not Hunt or Attwood but Grey, not Bright but Disraeli, not Chamberlain but Salisbury and Gladstone, not Pankhurst but Lloyd George designed the reform acts; and as politicians they designed them to benefit their own interests and, in general, their own parties. Whichever party initiated reform did so, at least in part, in order to gain from it. Electoral reform was undoubtedly part of the long-term party-political struggle for power.

Was it a principled struggle, as the Whig historians implied? Perhaps not. Consider, for example, Disraeli's *volte-face* over reform in 1867. It is very tempting to see politicians as unscrupulous and unprincipled power-seekers adopting the language of democracy merely to remain in office. Perhaps reforms were judicious concessions by the ruling elite to perpetuate its dominance for as long as possible and to avoid the truly democratic demands of the radicals. Were reforms initiated to prevent more extensive reforms? Were electoral reforms, in fact, merely cynical attempts to buy votes? The overall effect of the series of reforms between 1832 and 1918 may have been to bring Britain within measurable distance of democracy, but this was not the intention of the policy-makers, except at the very end of the period. On the contrary, many of the reforms of the period were specifically designed to avoid, rather than to hasten, democracy.

The evolution of democracy was therefore largely unintended and, in this sense, accidental, a view which makes Whig interpretations seem naive, if not indeed wildly idealistic.

Clearly many politicians paid only lip-service to democratic ideals. Even after 1918 there were those who longed, secretly, for a return to the good old days when it had not been necessary to beg the votes of the masses; and before this date 'democracy' remained, for the majority of politicians, a dirty word. Very few MPs wanted universal suffrage, and not many wanted even universal manhood suffrage. The idea that all men, even those receiving poor relief, should be able to vote was hotly repudiated by every government in the nineteenth century. But, even so, many politicians did take ideals seriously: they may not, generally, have believed in full democracy, but they did sincerely advocate 'liberty' and 'representative government'. The conviction that governments derived their legitimacy from the consent of the people – or at least from a large proportion of them – was becoming more and more firmly rooted as the twentieth century approached. To this extent, political principles were transformed during the nineteenth century. Whereas, at the start of the century, the onus had been on reformers to make out a convincing case for extending the vote, towards the end of the century the onus was on a small embattled minority to justify the status quo. Most politicians began to take for granted that the franchise should be widened. Gradually Tom Paine's view that people have a 'natural right' to vote had come to be accepted. It is therefore probably true to say that, if the Whig interpretation of history is unconvincingly idealistic, the notion that democracy resulted solely from the selfish manoeuvres of undemocratic politicians is unduly cynical.

Summary Diagram
Parliamentary Reform after 1832

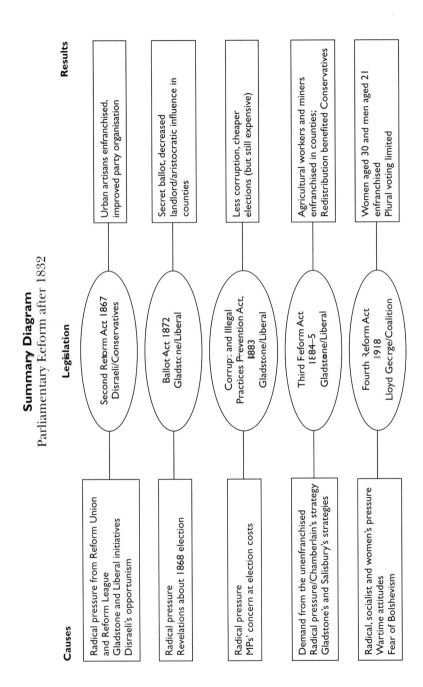

Causes

Radical pressure from Reform Union and Reform League
Gladstone and Liberal initiatives
Disraeli's opportunism

Radical pressure
Revelations about 1868 election

Radical pressure
MPs' concern at election costs

Demand from the unenfranchised
Radical pressure/Chamberlain's strategy
Gladstone's and Salisbury's strategies

Radical, socialist and women's pressure
Wartime attitudes
Fear of Bolshevism

Legislation

Second Reform Act 1867
Disraeli/Conservatives

Ballot Act 1872
Gladstone/Liberal

Corrupt and Illegal Practices Prevention Act, 1883
Gladstone/Liberal

Third Reform Act 1884–5
Gladstone/Liberal

Fourth Reform Act 1918
Lloyd George/Coalition

Results

Urban artisans enfranchised, improved party organisation

Secret ballot, decreased landlord/aristocratic influence in counties

Less corruption, cheaper elections (but still expensive)

Agricultural workers and miners enfranchised in counties; Redistribution benefited Conservatives

Women aged 30 and men aged 21 enfranchised
Plural voting limited

Working on Chapter 4

This chapter covers a long period and many important issues (as well as several examination topics). Do not be put off by this: make your notes section by section, one after another, and you will find that the material is easily manageable. Try to build your notes round three issues for each of the topics covered: (i) the causes of legislation, (ii) its content and (iii) its consequences. Such a systematic approach should make for clarity. It is also worthwhile pausing at the end of each reform and making a note of what was not changed, as well as of what was. In the final, concluding section, you should try to compare the importance of the various reform measures and identify whether they have a common set of causes. Is the importance of 'pressures', 'politicians' and 'principles' the same for each reform? If not, do their variations form any recognisable pattern? Don't be afraid to formulate your own views, rather than merely accepting those given here.

Answering structures and essay questions on Chapter 4

The period 1833–1918 is extremely broad, and therefore a wide variety of essay questions can be set. Sometimes questions are focused specifically on a single reform, in which case you will need to be selective about the material you include. But even a very 'narrow' question can be illuminated by your wider knowledge of the period as a whole: only a knowledge of the broad sweep of parliamentary reform will enable you to appreciate the context of a single issue and to see it in historical perspective. Alternatively, questions can address the whole process of reform. (In these wider questions, you should be able, from the material in this chapter, to write a paragraph or two on women's suffrage. For questions solely on this issue, however, you would need to read more widely. Paula Bartley's *Votes for Women*, in the *Access In Depth* series, is highly recommended.)

Consider the following structured question:

1 **a)** What were Disraeli's intentions in introducing a reform bill in 1866? (*5 marks*)
   b) What were the main reforms introduced by the Second Reform Act? (*10 marks*)
   c) 'A brilliant triumph for Disraeli.' Discuss this view of the Second Reform Act. (*20 marks*)

Do look carefully at the mark-scheme for this question. You will have a limited amount of time at your disposal, and it would be very easy to spend far too long on part a) and, especially, on b). So always read the parts of a structured question carefully, and allot your time sensibly, before beginning your answer. Clearly your answers to the first two sub-questions will contribute to your answer to the third – but what fresh issues would you introduce in c)? Perhaps Disraeli's succeeding to the leadership of the Conservative party and the effects of the Act on the party's electoral fortunes?

Consider also the following essay titles:

1. 'More concerned to stave off democracy than to bring it nearer'. Discuss with reference to at least one of the Reform Acts after 1832.
2. What was the significance of the legislation between 1865 and 1885 which made the system of government in Britain more democratic?
3. How significant were the Second and Third Reform Acts in the achievement of democracy in Britain?
4. What was expected and what was actually achieved by the 1867 Reform Act?
5. To what extent did the reforms enacted in 1884–5 establish British government on a popular basis?

Note how all of these titles demand a wider knowledge than that of any single reform act: even those that ask specifically about one reform require some understanding of politics before and after that one piece of legislation. Question 5, for instance, asks about the Third Reform Act, and yet it can only be answered satisfactorily if you make comparisons with the Second and Fourth Reform Acts.

It is worthwhile constructing essay plans for as many of these questions as possible. Be certain to pinpoint the exact meaning of each question. Determine, for instance, whether you are being asked about the causes or the consequences of the reforms, or whether both are equally important. It is also important to be clear about which reforms are relevant, especially in question 2, where no precise Acts are mentioned. Remember the importance of devising suitable themes for each of the middle paragraphs. There is no 'right' way of doing this. For question 4, for instance, would you have separate paragraphs on the expectations of the reformers, followed by a set of paragraphs on the achievements of the Act? Such a structure might work well. On the other hand, you might have thematic paragraphs on particular issues – like the prevention of public disturbances, the strengthening of the Tory Party, the preservation of the existing system in the counties, etc – in which you discuss both aims and results. This is a more direct approach and might well produce a better, more sophisticated essay. Yet it is probably more difficult to manage. Each student should adopt the structure he or she feels most confident at handling. The essential thing, however, is that you have a coherent plan.

Source-based questions on Chapter 4

1. Gladstone and Lowe on the Liberal Reform Bill, 1866
Read the extracts from the speeches by William Gladstone and Robert Lowe on pages 56 and 58, and answer the following questions:

a) Explain what was meant by a '£7 franchise' in Gladstone's speech (line 1). (*1 mark*)

b) Why do you think Gladstone disliked the prospect of 'the peasantry' and 'mere hand labour' (line 4) having the vote? (*3 marks*)

c) Gladstone referred to the new voters as 'recruits to your army' (line 14). Why do you think he used this particular phrase? (*4 marks*)

d) In Lowe's speech, what 'causes' were at work tending to 'multiply the franchise' (lines 2 and 3)? (*2 marks*)

e) What does Lowe imply would be the consequences of working men awakening to 'a full sense of their power' (lines 15–16)? (*4 marks*)

f) What differences and what similarities are there between the two speeches? Do the latter outweigh the former? (*9 marks*)

2. 'The Derby, 1867'
Study the cartoon from *Punch*, 25 May, 1867, on page 62, and answer the following questions:

a) In what sense is this depiction of the Reform Bill issue as a race an apt one? (*4 marks*)

b) What do you think the cartoonist was trying to convey about Disraeli's motives by the way he has portrayed him? Explain your answer. (*5 marks*)

c) What is the significance of Mr Punch's suspicious comment? (*6 marks*)

3. Two politicians on corrupt practices
Read the extracts on pages 67 and 68, and answer the following questions:

a) Drawing evidence from the content and style of the extracts, say how far you think the two politicians disapproved of the practices they described. (*5 marks*)

b) Basing your answer on the extracts, and also on your wider knowledge, estimate how widespread were the practices described here. (*10 marks*)

5 Local Government

POINTS TO CONSIDER

This chapter introduces you to the transformation of local government that occurred in Victorian Britain, in both counties and boroughs. You need to become familiar with the evolving pattern of local authorities and with the work they undertook. Remember the degree of variation that existed throughout the country, and do not imagine that national legislation affected all authorities equally. Finally, try to see the connections between local government and the changes in national government covered in the previous two chapters.

KEY DATES

1835 Municipal Corporations Act.
1848 Public Health Act, allowing local sanitary boards to be set up.
1871 Local Government Board was set up.
1873 Joseph Chamberlain became Lord Mayor of Birmingham.
1875 Public Health Act, codifying over 30 previous Acts.
1882 Municipal Corporations Act, removing restrictions on local authority services.
1888 Local Government Act, setting up county councils.
1894 Local Government act, setting up district councils.

Local government is been badly neglected in most general surveys of Victorian history. There are several reasons for this. While national politics seem important and exciting, local government is often dismissed – quite unfairly – as trivial and tedious. But perhaps the most vital reason is the sheer difficulty of making sense of the enormously complicated structures of local government in this period. There are few generalisations that hold true about nineteenth-century local administration. Certainly there was no straightforward system; and most reforms tended only to diversify an already bewildering pattern. As a result, few have penetrated beyond the complex structures of local government to examine the work that was performed.

This conspiracy of silence is much to be regretted. We should not avoid issues merely because they are complicated, and we must study local government for the very good reason that it was vitally important. The Victorians themselves gave far more emphasis to local, rather than national, issues. Indeed they were often acutely suspicious of Whitehall. Centralisation, wrote one commentator in 1851, was synonymous with 'irresponsible control; meddling interference; and arbitrary taxation': it was simply 'Communism in another form'. What they termed 'local self-government', however, was much more to their liking: being decentralised, it was closer to the people and easier to control. Most government in the nineteenth century was in fact local rather than national. The general rule was that what could be done by local authorities should be done by them, and not by the central government. Thus far more people participated in local rather than national politics: the local franchises tended to be wider, and women became voters in local elections, and indeed took office as councillors, several decades before they could elect Members of Parliament. Certainly people's lives were vitally affected by local institutions. Local government could literally be a matter of life or death, as standards of health depended far more on local public health measures than the prescriptions of Whitehall politicians.

1 The Structures of Local Government before 1832

> **KEY ISSUES** Why did local government at this time have such a varied and diverse pattern, and why were changes thought to be necessary?

The form of local government before the Great Reform Act was very complicated. No one would have deliberately built such a patchwork of varied authorities – and indeed no one had done so. Local government had simply evolved over the centuries from feudal times, producing what one historian has called a veritable 'museum of constitutional archaeology'. Central government exercised very little control, and provided no grants to support local government, the revenue for local administration being raised from local taxes ('the rates') on local property. Many idealists would have liked to sweep away old forms and to start again, building efficient and rational structures from scratch. But their aims were impractical. The reforms that were introduced tended to be piecemeal and of local origin, incremental changes built onto what already existed, and to vary from place to place, thus making the overall pattern ever more elaborate.

Basically, local government in Britain comprised a two-tier structure of councils, at the county and parish levels. The parish (originally 'that circuit of ground which the souls under the care of one parson or vicar do inhabit') was in fact the basic building block of administration. There were around 15,000 parishes in England and Wales, each of which was controlled by its own council, the vestry (named after the church room in which parish business was conducted). It was established in Tudor times that every parish should have four officers: a churchwarden (concerned with the church and graveyard), a constable (to maintain law and order), a surveyor of highways (to keep roads in repair) and an overseer of the poor (in charge of poor relief). The tier of administration above the parish was the county, over which presided a Lord Lieutenant, who was generally one of the leading landowners in the area. However, the Lord Lieutenant, who was appointed by the Crown, tended to be a figurehead. The active administrators were the Justices of the Peace (JPs), about 5,000 of them in 1832, who were appointed on the Lord Lieutenant's recommendation to be in overall charge of groups of parishes. The JPs were important local figures, often squires or Anglican clergymen. Not only did they levy rates and supervise the work of the parishes, they were also magistrates, presiding over special courts ('Quarter Sessions') four times a year.

There was an important exception to this two-tier (parish–county) structure. Some, though not all, of Britain's towns had been given the status of boroughs, often because a royal charter had been granted to them, allowing them to run their own affairs. Though they would be divided into separate parishes, in such places the upper tier of administration was provided by the borough council, known as a municipal corporation.

So far this seems very orderly, and easily understood: it sounds, in fact, very much like a system! Yet this basic structure was marked by many exceptions and variations. There were, in some parts of the country, other institutions, such as 'manorial courts leet and courts baron', judicial bodies which had survived from medieval times. Some towns, such as Canterbury and Norwich, were themselves legally designated counties. On the other hand, some towns were not even designated as boroughs, while some boroughs were too small to be considered real towns. And even within the basic two-tier system (parish–county or parish–borough) there were many differences from one area to another. Parishes, for instance, varied enormously in size, in population, and in efficiency. In Suffolk the average parish was around 2 square miles, while in Northumberland it was 12, and one parish in Lancashire covered 161 square miles. Similarly, parishes could have a few inhabitants or 200,000. All parishes were legally obliged to have four officers, but in practice not all did so; and since these officers were unpaid, they tackled their work with varying degrees of (in)competence. Rural parishes were more likely to be efficient than urban ones, but almost everywhere constables and surveyors of highways had ceased to exercise any real function by the end of the eighteenth century. Some, though not all, officers became corrupt. Bethnal Green, in London, was notoriously the most corrupt parish in the country.

Vestries also varied. All the inhabitants of a parish theoretically had the right to participate in parochial business; and there were some 'open' vestries, which were among the most democratic – and rowdy – institutions in the country. But in practice 'close' or 'select' vestries, in which an oligarchy of local bigwigs had taken over control of parish affairs, had become the typical form of parish government by the early-nineteenth century.

Similarly, the quality of the JPs and their work was anything but uniform. Despite the fact that they were unpaid, the JPs' work was really very onerous. Originally responsible for justice and law and order, they soon had to administer the poor law, to control alcohol, pave, light and cleanse thoroughfares, and numerous other duties. Not being superhuman, they were unable to perform all aspects of their work satisfactorily.

Many municipal corporations, especially those elected on a very limited franchise, were grossly negligent and inefficient: indeed some – dubbed 'chartered hogsties' by *The Times* – seemed to believe that their sole *raison d'être* was to choose MPs. However, others were more progressive and petitioned parliament for extra powers, which were granted through local acts of parliament. These enabled local authorities to set up special agencies, often referred to as 'ad hoc bodies', to tackle particular problems: for example, Incorporated Guardians of the Poor, to improve poor relief; Turnpike Trusts, to construct and maintain roads and levy tolls on traffic for their upkeep; and Improvement Commissions, which usually each tackled one problem, such as drainage, water supply, policing or the paving or lighting of streets. No fewer than 300 special bodies were set up like this in the 30 years after 1800. However, while some of them were relatively efficient, others were decidedly inefficient and corrupt. Another problem was that commissions often had overlapping duties, so that there was rivalry between them. Lancaster had two drainage commissions, which would not co-operate with each other. Nevertheless, such bodies were among the most promising developments in local government in the years before 1832, especially since they could be introduced in all towns, not merely incorporated ones. They showed that there was a degree of flexibility within unreformed local government. Yet they created almost as many problems as they solved, and they certainly complicated the nationwide pattern of local government.

a) The Need for Change

By 1832 reformers were adamant that fundamental changes were needed. Whereas the local government system (if that word be allowed) had been built up in earlier centuries, nineteenth-century Britain was the scene of major socio-economic changes, including population growth. The population of England and Wales doubled between 1801 and 1851. Many parishes began to burst at the seams, due to population growth and an influx of migrants, while others had a declining population. Similarly, many boroughs now had fewer inhabitants, whereas numerous growing towns were not recognised as boroughs and had to muddle along – at great human cost – within the old parish–county structure, with the addition, in some areas, of improvement commissioners. JPs, who had done a reasonable job in earlier times, were often loath to administer these new towns. An eighteenth-century journalist reported that 'gentlemen' would not serve as Justices in areas 'inhabited by the scum and dregs of the people'. Such urban areas witnessed poverty, squalor and poor health, and also dramatically rising crime rates. London's Metropolitan Police had been set up at Scotland Yard in 1829, but other areas were very slow to set up efficient police forces, despite the fact that the success of the Metropolitan force tended to drive criminals out of London into the rest of the country. It seemed to many observers that the old system could not cope with the new demands of an industrialising Britain. By the early 1830s a thorough reform of the system seemed long overdue.

2 Reform in the 1830s and 1840s

> **KEY ISSUE** Why were reforms in local administration so tentative in these decades?

The Great Reform Act of 1832 did not stabilise the old political system so much as whet the appetite for further change, and certainly local government could not fail to be affected. Surely the 'rotten boroughs', many of which had now been disfranchised, could not be expected to continue as institutions of local administration for much longer. Nor were the other boroughs deemed to be satisfactory: some were 'close' corporations, basically self-electing oligarchies, and even the 'open' ones often discriminated against non-Anglicans and were indifferent to good administration. And, of course, many of the country's largest towns did not even enjoy borough status. Reformers demanded important changes to the structure of local government institutions, wishing in particular to see the introduction of representative local councils.

a) The Municipal Corporations Act, 1835

An enquiry into municipal corporations was set up in 1833. Historians are generally agreed that the commission tended to attribute the corruption of the worst corporations to most of them; but in the 3,446 pages of the report there were many examples of flagrant abuses.

The outcome was the Municipal Corporations Act of 1835, which was to apply both to existing boroughs in England and Wales and to towns which petitioned for borough status in the future. (Scotland had already been subject to similar legislation in 1833.) The Act called for the election of unpaid local councillors every three years as a municipal corporation to represent the local community. The councillors would then elect a mayor and aldermen from among their number. All those who had paid rates for three years might vote in the election. Council meetings were now to be open to the public, and local accounts were to be audited once a year to prevent corruption. Local councils were also to have paid officials (at least a town clerk and a borough treasurer) and were empowered to make by-laws, set up a police force and levy rates. Furthermore, they could undertake many more functions, including the provision of public baths and wash-houses, libraries and lunatic asylums. They could, in fact, take over the duties of local improvement commissions if they so chose. Finally, the Act specified that justice was to be separated from administration: the latter would be the responsibility of the council, while the former would be the responsibility of magistrates appointed by the Crown.

The Act was certainly a landmark in the growth of urban local government, putting more of the work of local administration on the shoulders of elected representatives. Yet it is important to recognise that it was not a thorough or particularly effective reform. It was applied to 178 old corporations, but not to all 246. London was omitted as being too large, and other places as too small. There was no rush for other towns to petition for borough status, and nor did it prove easy for them to do so successfully. By 1861 only 29 new boroughs had been created (a figure that grew to 62 by 1876). It seems, on balance, that it created a wider franchise for local elections than the 1832 Reform Act did for parliamentary contests; but the ratepayer qualification undoubtedly ruled out the bulk of the population, since only a small minority owned property and so paid rates. Those who rented property, and whose rates would be included in their rent, were not entitled to vote, and all women were expressly excluded. In addition, only very wealthy men, owning property to the value of £1,000 (or £500 in smaller boroughs), were eligible to stand for election. The result was that the impact of the measure was anything but uniform, with major changes to the composition of corporations in some towns, including Leicester and Norwich, but only minor alterations in others, such as Nottingham (where the new arrangements actually reduced the number of electors) and Exeter.

There was also considerable variation in how the new law was operated. This was only to be expected since, though it empowered councils to do much, it actually required them to do little. And, since most local councillors were men of substance whose first aim was to keep down the rates, there was a tendency to avoid expensive projects. Few councils decided to replace improvement commissions, being content instead to work alongside such bodies. In short, the legislation made urban government more representative (of the wealthier elements), and paved the way for party political contests, but it was more concerned with the form of local authorities than with the substance of what they did. In a majority of boroughs, it did only a little to make municipal government more efficient and professional. Yet at least it was a start.

b) The Poor Law Amendment Act, 1834

Another major legislative enactment affecting local government had reached the statute book a year earlier, in 1834. For years successive governments had been alarmed at the escalating costs of poor law relief and at how this money was being spent. What seemed an unduly high proportion was going to augment the wages of labourers in the south of England. House-owners and landowners were aggrieved at the escalating rates and *laissez-faire* thinkers decided that, with such subsidies from ratepayers to employers, the free market economy could not function properly. In 1832 a commission investigated the system. It criticised the enormous variations in methods of poor relief between parishes and concluded that 'Every penny bestowed, that tends to render the condition of the pauper more eligible than that of the independent labourer is a bounty on indolence and vice'. The commissioners decided therefore that relief in aid of wages should be stopped completely: able-bodied people who applied for poor relief should be compelled to enter the workhouse. The threat of the workhouse ('the local Bastille') would be the incentive that people needed to find decently paid employment. The result, so it was hoped, would be a smaller expenditure on poor relief and the reinvigoration of the whole economy. Admittedly those in the workhouse might suffer, but in a good cause, for the end result would be that consummation so devoutly wished by utilitarians, 'the greatest happiness of the greatest number – (see page 33 for the utilitarian philosophy).

The new Act was not in fact fully implemented. There was so much resistance to its provisions that in the north and the midlands 'outdoor relief', as opposed to the 'indoor' (workhouse) relief, continued to be given. Nevertheless the Act was of profound importance for local government. The old system, with relief provided in every parish by the overseer of the poor or, increasingly, by local Incorporated Guardians of the Poor, was now ended. Instead, the Act set up a central authority, a three-man Poor Law Commission with power to group the parishes into larger, more cost-effective units or 'unions', each of which was to have a workhouse and in each of which a board of guardians, elected by local ratepayers, would levy a special rate and be responsible for poor relief. It thus created the first central government institution with responsibility for an aspect of local government, so that the Poor Law Commission may be seen as the forerunner, even if a tentative one, of what later became a full-scale ministry. It also introduced a fundamental change into the structure of local government. 15,000 parishes were soon grouped into 700 unions, which, by disregarding county and borough boundaries, cut across existing local structures. Furthermore, the boards of guardians constituted the first elective local government institutions to cover the whole country, both counties and boroughs. Whatever its effect on poor relief, the act of 1834 certainly reformed – but complicated – the structure and finances of local government.

c) Public Health Act, 1848

Public health was a key force driving local government reform. This was a period of significant urbanisation – the census for 1851 was to show that, for the first time, a majority of the population in England and Wales lived in towns – and if urban Britons were to be kept alive, government had to react constructively. The deteriorating standards of health in towns had been remarked upon by the Poor Law Commission, and in 1842 its secretary, Edwin Chadwick, published the *Sanitary Condition of the Labouring Population of Great Britain*, a graphic exposé of the squalor, overcrowding and unhygienic conditions that existed in urban Britain, establishing, for instance, that over 57 per cent of those born of the 'labouring classes' in Manchester died before the age of five years. Average life expectancy was twice as great in Wiltshire as in Liverpool. Filth, argued Chadwick, killed far more Britons than war. Having started with the common Victorian prejudice that fecklessness produced poverty, he ended by concluding that illness, stemming from poor social conditions, was a major cause. Chadwick therefore argued that local authorities should be instructed to carry out a whole range of reforms, from improved housing to better sanitation and drainage. His prescription was not so much curative as preventive, more a matter of engineering than of medicine.

Many disliked Chadwick, finding him arrogant and pompous. Still more viewed his recommendations with suspicion, as smacking of dangerous centralising tendencies. But the weight of evidence in favour of action against the spread of disease was overwhelming. There was widespread fear of cholera and plague – the cholera epidemic of 1848–9 killed around 62,000 – and in this atmosphere the Public Health Act of 1848 was passed. It set up a General Board of Health in Whitehall, with powers to institute local sanitary boards in areas where local ratepayers petitioned for one or where the annual death rate consistently exceeded the national average of 23 per 1,000. Such boards would take over responsibility for improved public health amenities: they could manage sewers and refuse systems, appoint a Medical Officer of Health, regulate slaughter houses, remove 'nuisances' and provide burial grounds – and they would have the power to levy local rates and purchase land.

Action was taken on public health. Yet it was extremely tentative. The 1848 Act, like so much legislation of this period, was *permissive* rather than *mandatory*: local authorities could set up boards of health if they so chose, and even then the boards would have discretion over which duties they undertook. The General Board's power to insist that councils set up local boards was never used. Most councils, composed of shopkeepers and businessmen whose main concern was to keep the rates as low as possible, were slow to act. Indeed there was a good deal of resentment at the promptings of the General Board, which was therefore disbanded in 1858. Nor did the new legislation have any noticeable impact on health standards in Britain's cities. Death rates across the country tended to rise in the period after 1848 for another decade or so. Nevertheless, in the longer term, progress was made. While only about 100 local boards, covering only one-fifteenth of the country, were established during the first decade of the Act, over 550 more were established in the second. In the 1870s almost every part of the country had its own local sanitary board, and so-called 'filth diseases' (caused by the fouling of water or food by infected excrement) declined markedly from the middle of this decade.

In addition, the legislation affected the form of local government. In municipal boroughs the town council usually became the local sanitary board, and the town itself was the 'sanitary area' in which the board had jurisdiction. Outside the towns, however, the union was usually, but not always, the 'sanitary area' and the board of guardians was generally recognised as the rural sanitary authority. Elsewhere special boards were elected by ratepayers. As hitherto, an extension of the work of local authorities tended to complicate the structure of local government.

3 Urban Local Government after mid-century

> **KEY ISSUE** How were towns governed around 1860?

Far more important than government legislation were the initiatives of local authorities themselves. Indeed the basic effect of the 1835 Municipal Corporations Act, as of the 1848 Public Health Act, had been to empower local authorities to take action if they so wished. Furthermore, local authorities still turned to private acts of parliament to set up special agencies to tackle particular problems. The result was that vigorous boroughs tended to get things done, while others stagnated. 'Go-slow' local authorities could generally get away with neglecting even the small range of duties which was technically compulsory. Liverpool and Manchester are good examples of progressive boroughs, while Barrow and Bury are often cited as examples of municipal backwardness.

Hence the national pattern of urban government was remarkably varied and confused. Indeed the administration of a single town might be equally chaotic. In the 1860s an individual might find himself subject to half a dozen separate local authorities, for each of which he might vote and to each of which he might have to pay a separate rate. There would be the traditional parish vestry, the board of guardians and the board of health (which might or might not be one and the same), as well as separate ad hoc bodies – the baths and washhouse board, the burial board, as well as sewage and drainage boards, the highway board and, from 1871, the school board (elected under the 1870 Education Act to levy rates for non-church schools). The existence of such a cluster of bodies would not have been so bad if the functions of the separate units had not overlapped so much. When the Medical Officer for Merthyr Tydfil was asked in 1869 who was responsible for public health, he replied: 'The local Board of Health, two Burial Boards, the Board of Guardians, the Superintendent and district Registrars, and the Inspector of Factories and his subordinates.' He could have added another – himself. In a single town, separate authorities might provide hospitals and ambulances, and a third be responsible for medical staff. Such fragmented structures almost inevitably tended to reduce the sense of individual responsibility for any given duty among employees and thereby to hinder efficiency.

No wonder George Goschen, the President of the Poor Law Board, exclaimed in 1871 that 'we have a chaos as regards authorities, a chaos as regards rates, and a worse chaos than all as regards areas'. His words were well chosen. There were a total of 27,069 local authorities of all kinds at this date, imposing 18 different kinds of rates. As for the areas of their jurisdiction, there were 52 counties of greatly varied size; 239 municipal boroughs showing even greater diversity of size and population; 1,500 sanitary districts, some with 100,000 people, some with 40; 2,051 school board districts; 649 Poor Law unions; as well as 424 highway districts and 853 burial board districts. And this is not a full list! Furthermore, these various authorities would be elected by equally varied franchises. There was a ratepayer franchise in the municipal boroughs, extended in 1869 to include the tenants of properties of sufficient rateable value, an important change that greatly increased the number of voters; but local boards of health and poor law guardians were elected on the basis of property values, so that the very wealthy might have up to six votes. Electors for school boards had as many votes as there were places to be filled and might give them all to one candidate or distribute them over a larger number.

4 Growth of Central Government's Role after 1870

> **KEY ISSUE** In what ways did central government intervene in local affairs?

The government's answer to this confusion was to set up a Local Government Board in 1871 to supervise local government and especially to spearhead improvements in public health. The national government was now taking a much more important role in local affairs. For instance, legislation now tended to be mandatory rather than merely permissive. The Sanitary Act of 1866 made it compulsory for local authorities to undertake sanitary regulation, although the means of enforcement were weak, and the Public Health Act of 1872 insisted that they appoint a Medical Officer of Health and provide a proper water supply. Another Public Health Act, in 1875, codified over 30 earlier pieces of legislation and clearly established exactly what duties local government had to perform. Greater administrative uniformity also came about. There was a revision of local areas and authorities, so that everywhere the town council or the board of guardians became the sanitary authority. Central government also allowed local authorities to take out loans: in 1873 alone local authorities borrowed almost £1 million for sanitary purposes. This injection of cash, together with a clearer realisation of the medical connection between disease and dirt, tended to overcome the initial reluctance of local councils to engage in large-scale water and sanitary improvements.

In many ways, finance was the crux of the matter. Local revenue from the rates increased significantly after 1830, but central government grants increased even more rapidly.

Local revenue from rates		Central government subsidy
1830	£8 million	£0
1870	£16 million	£1.25 million
1900	£40 million	£12 million

With the rise in government grants came a gradual increase in the central control of how the money was spent. The first important grant came in 1856: the Exchequer would pay one-quarter of police pay and uniform costs, a sum that might be withheld if the police were inefficient. Other grants were similarly conditional. Grants from the school board, for instance, required regular government inspections of the subsidised schools in order to maintain standards. But even so, local government remained largely independent. There was prompting rather than dictation from Whitehall, and most local authorities by the 1870s needed no such pressure. The initiative for improvements still lay primarily in the cities.

5 The Era of Civic Pride

KEY ISSUE How did the administration of Britain's cities develop in the last third of the century?

A sense of solidarity and pride amongst the inhabitants of particular cities had been apparent before the middle of the century. Councils attempted to develop a civic identity by means of a new elaborate ritual and ceremony on civic occasions, by the construction of grand town halls and other public buildings and by the provision of public parks. Rivalry between towns, as with Leeds and Bradford, also stimulated improvement schemes. Certainly, by the 1860s, the central parts of many British cities had become more splendid as well as tidier. But perhaps the best example of civic pride leading to a greatly improved urban environment came in the rapidly growing city of Birmingham in the 1870s, stemming from the city's 1861 Improvement Act and being informed by a spirit of evangelical dissent which identified urban improvement with morality. Historians have singled out the role of R.W. Dale, a nonconformist minister in Birmingham from 1845 to 1895, in developing this 'civic gospel'. Dale believed that local authorities

1 can do much to improve those miserable homes which are fatal not only to health, but to decency and morality. They can give to the poor the enjoyment of pleasant parks and gardens, and the intellectual cultivation and refinement of public libraries and galleries of art. They can
5 redress in many ways the inequalities of human conditions. The gracious words of Christ, 'Inasmuch as ye did it unto one of these my brethren, ye did it unto Me' will be addressed not only to those who with their own hands fed the hungry, and clothed the naked, and cared for the sick, but to those who supported a municipal policy which lessened the
10 miseries of the wretched and added brightness to the life of the desolate.

Above all, Dale was determined that good works should be practical. The eleventh commandment, he insisted, is that 'thou shalt keep a balance sheet'.

a) Birmingham and Joe Chamberlain

The movement reached its peak when Joseph Chamberlain, a successful screw manufacturer, became Mayor of Birmingham in 1873. Birmingham had not been a city renowned for being progressive. On the contrary, under pressure from Westminster, it had only just appointed a Medical Officer of Health. Over the previous decades the town council had proved remarkably economical, meeting in a local pub rather than pay the construction costs of a proper debating chamber.

In 1873 Chamberlain had been a councillor for only four years but was already a nationally known figure. He had the right religious connections: almost every mayor had been a Unitarian since the town's incorporation in 1839. He also had the support of a Liberal-dominated town council. With these assets, he aimed to improve both housing and public health, and thereby, in his own words, to encourage 'a sense of the importance and dignity of municipal life'.

His first major project was to buy Birmingham's gas companies. The purchase of local gas companies by a town council was, by this time, nothing new in Britain. By 1870, 49 corporations produced and sold their own gas supply, thus participating in what became known as 'municipal trading'. What marked Chamberlain out was a determination to run such concerns profitably. Indeed, in the course of debate he offered himself to rent the gas undertaking from the corporation at £20,000 a year, guaranteeing to make a personal fortune within a decade. His confidence was soon vindicated. Over the next five years, the price of gas to consumers was twice reduced but profits for the council turned out to be even higher than predicted, allowing Chamberlain to pay for parks, museums and general civic improvements, including a 'handsome and commodious Council Chamber'. In addition, he set up Birmingham's first health committee, charged with the disposal of sewage and the inspection of water. The result was a 20 per cent fall in the city's death rate

In his second term of office, with the passing of a special local act, he undertook a vast slum clearance programme in 50 acres of some of the most squalid areas of the city. The showpiece of the redeveloped site was a vast new thoroughfare – named, appropriately enough, Corporation Street – designed to bear comparison with the centre of any other city in the country. The cost was high, around £1.5 million, but to bear such sums would, insisted Chamberlain, be a policy of 'sagacious audacity'. He estimated that, with the enhanced rateable value of new commercial premises, the burden on the rates would be quite manageable. He was correct. Even so, the clearance of slums did not create new houses, with the result that many working-class families could not find the decent accommodation the mayor knew they needed. Overcrowding was the problem of the late nineteenth-century city, and municipal government came nowhere near to solving it. Nevertheless Chamberlain had made Birmingham a model for other towns. Only election to the House of Commons in 1876 ended his reforming zeal in local government, and by this time he was able to boast that the city had been 'parked, paved, assized, marketed, Gas-and-Watered and improved'. In 1890 an American writer clearly agreed with him, calling Birmingham 'the best-governed city in the world'.

b) London and the Fabians

In 1880 an act of parliament made any householder eligible for election as a local councillor, and two years later the Municipal Corporations Act removed the last restrictions on the services that local authorities might undertake. The result was the emergence of a new type of councillor willing to undertake a greater variety of local activities than even Chamberlain had contemplated. Nowhere was this more true than in the capital. London had long been an exception in British local government, primarily because of its size. It also had a reputation for corrupt and inadequate local administration. But in 1888 the London County Council (LCC) was formed and, under its authority, London soon overtook Birmingham as the most progressive council in the country.

Whereas many large councils saw party political battles between Conservatives and Liberals, the LCC from the first saw a contest between looser alignments of 'progressives' and 'moderates'. The former, who achieved control in 1889, included Fabian socialists like Sidney Webb, as well as a number of radical Conservatives. As a result, the new council became the first in the country to build its own housing estates. 'Municipal trading' was taken much further than anywhere else. Webb described the results:

1 The individualist town councillor will walk along the municipal pavement, lit by municipal gas and cleansed by municipal brooms with municipal water and – seeing by the municipal clock in the municipal market, that he is too early to meet his children coming from the
5 municipal school, hard by the county lunatic asylum and the municipal hospital, will use the national telegraph system to tell them not to walk through the municipal park, but to come by the municipal tramway to meet him in the municipal reading-room, by the municipal museum, art-gallery and library ...

Men such as Webb were often criticised by revolutionary socialists as mere 'gas and water' reformers. But they responded with an insistence that schemes of municipal reform were not only immensely important and beneficial, but that they embodied a practical form of socialism.

6 Rural Local Government after mid-century

> **KEY ISSUES** How did county government develop? Why did democratisation come more slowly than in the towns?

After the 1835 Municipal Corporations Act, reformers had wanted to see the replacement of the paternal and sometimes inefficient administration of the JPs by elected councils. Landowning MPs had vetoed their proposals. But the JPs' work had been curtailed by the Poor Law Act of 1834 and by public health acts from 1848 onwards, and their days looked numbered. Already changes were occurring in the composition of the magistracy, as new men began to be appointed. In 1867–77 16 per cent of new magistrates were middle-class, rather than landowners; and in the following decade 30 per cent of new appointees were middle-class men. The trend was towards a broadening of the background from which JPs came. After the Reform Act of 1884, which extended the vote to two million agricultural labourers, reform of county government could not be long delayed.

a) Local Government Act, 1888

Reform was undertaken in 1888 by the Conservative government of Lord Salisbury. The Local Government Act's main provision was that the administrative powers of the JPs in England and Wales were to be transferred to county councils elected on a householder franchise. (Similar legislation was drafted for Scotland the following year.) This was a significant reform, but it seems likely that the Conservatives sponsored it in order to forestall still greater changes. Under their legislation, for instance, the JPs would not only remain as magistrates but would have joint control, along with the county councils, of the police. In addition, the new bodies would not be responsible for the provision of expensive poor law relief, which was retained by the local guardians, even though they took over the functions of many other local boards and commissions. Furthermore, the framers of the bill had proposed that only the 10 towns with a population of over 100,000 should be excluded from the administrative authority of the county councils. In this way, the sway of what were hoped to be relatively conservative bodies would extend widely over the whole country. However, the Bill was amended in committee so that, in the end, 57 boroughs with a population of over 50,000 were excluded, together with 4 having less than 50,000. Hence 61 towns were given the status of 'county boroughs' and were entirely outside the jurisdiction of the county councils, and other towns could achieve this status once they had reached a population of 50,000.

Nevertheless, Conservative aims were largely realised. The political status of landowners in the counties was altered by the legislation, but their decline was slow and incomplete. Many JPs found it relatively easy to secure election as county councillors, so that, after the first elections under the new law, just over half of the new councillors were magistrates. For several decades the new county councils were filled with men – country gentlemen, clergymen, professionals and farmers – who had previously dominated the Quarter Sessions, though in Wales and Scotland the magistrates were very much in a minority.

The Act was clearly flawed. While extending the powers of the local authorities, so that county councils took over responsibility for roads, bridges and lunatic asylums, as well as the administrative work of the JPs, there was no real attempt to ensure that they administered a conveniently sized area or indeed that they had the revenue (from the rates) to do the work they were supposed to do. Whereas a new administrative county was created for the London area (the LCC), there was no thorough attempt to reform the units of county government. County boundaries owed more to the Anglo-Saxons and Normans than to rational political science. Continuity therefore triumphed over efficiency. For instance, Rutland retained its county status, despite a population of only 21,000, compared to an average for all counties of 500,000 – and Lancashire had 3,450,000 people. Yorkshire and Lincolnshire were sub-divided, but otherwise the historic counties were accepted as units of county administration.

b) Local Government Act, 1894

In 1894 a new Local Government Act reformed the authorities below county or county borough level, establishing a system of district councils, in both rural and urban areas, to take over the duties of the sanitary authorities and the local government and highway boards. The confusion of multiple separate bodies, going back to the Improvement Commissions of the eighteenth century, was, at least, much simplified. The rural districts were generally the old poor law unions, while urban councils were generally the smaller towns, though some of them were absurdly small: Childwall In Lancashire had only 219 inhabitants. Even so, at least provision was made that rural and urban district councils should not cut across country or county borough boundaries.

The vote for the new councils was given to all those who could vote in parliamentary or county council elections. The whole of the local government system was thus based on popular direct election. The Act also revitalised the parish system. A parish council was to be elected for every parish with a population of over 300, or for smaller parishes if a council was requested. Yet their powers of levying rates were much restricted, and so they were able to undertake only relatively minor, inexpensive duties.

The division of functions and responsibilities between, on the one hand, the county or county borough council and, on the other, the subordinate rural or urban district councils, was not clearly defined. Therefore there was often friction between the two sets of bodies. Nevertheless, at least the legislation of 1894 had created a regular two-tier form of local administration in Britain.

7 Conclusion: Local Government around 1900

> **KEY ISSUE** How significant were the changes that occurred in local government over the century?

Local government was still in the process of evolution by 1900. But a pattern had emerged. There had been major changes in the structure of local authorities, in the work that they undertook, in their relationship with central government, in the way they were chosen and thus in their composition, and in their professionalism.

a) Structure

The variety amounting to chaos that had characterised local administration at the start of the century had been replaced by a true system of local government by 1900. This is not to say that there was still no variety, and some confusion, for there certainly was. Tidy-minded administrators were still appalled at variations in the size and resources of the different bodies. The allocation of duties as between county (or county borough) and district was also a cause of considerable friction. But at least the all-purpose councils had replaced the separate, overlapping ad hoc bodies and agencies. In 1902 the school boards were abolished, and their duties undertaken by the local authorities. Only the Poor Law guardians lived on as separate entities within the local government system, surviving until 1929. The structure of local government had been changed fundamentally.

b) Duties

What stands out most, perhaps, about the work of local government by the end of the nineteenth century was its extent. It was responsible not just for law and order and the relief of poverty, but for public health (including sewage disposal, water supply and hospital provision), education, the management of rivers, and many other duties. It is not surprising, therefore, that the nineteenth century was marked by the progressive increase of local government expenditure: from just over £5 million in 1803 to around £29 million in 1870 and £67 million in 1893. In 1911 the figure was almost £140 million. Also noteworthy was the degree to which local bodies engaged in municipal trading, providing not only gas and water but also electricity and transport. In 1901 61 local authorities ran their own tramways. Doncaster's ran its own racecourse, and Glasgow's its telephone service. The total receipts accruing to local authorities from such services grew from £3 million in 1880 to £40 million in 1913. All local authorities had to undertake a minimum number of statutory tasks; but they could also opt for extra duties, still undertaken as a result of local acts of parliament. In 1900 alone 291 such acts were passed. Hence Rochdale was able to control the local ice-cream trade, and Leeds to regulate the city's brothels. As for the efficiency of local government activities, there were substantial variations from place to place.

c) Autonomy

As the duties of the local authorities became more extensive, so did the supervision of the central government. Local government thus had far less autonomy at the end of the century than at its beginning. This was partly due to Parliament's insistence, through mandatory legislation from the 1860s onwards, that the local authorities had to undertake particular tasks, and also to the greater provision of grants from the central government. Grants-in-aid, to use their technical name, grew from £12 million in 1900 to £21 million in 1913. But there was little friction between national and local government; and if citizens of 1800 would have been shocked and dismayed by the degree to which the central government interfered in local affairs, what strikes observers now is the wide degree of independence enjoyed by councillors in 1900 compared with the situation today. It became established that local authorities were the main agencies by which central government introduced changes, and that, as elected bodies in their own right, they could have considerable latitude in the way they did so. Only the legislation of 1911, which set up national insurance schemes for unemployment and ill health, thus by-passing the local authorities, began to depart from this principle.

d) Election and Composition

In 1835 it was uncertain whether the municipal council franchise was more liberal than that for borough elections to Westminster. Thereafter local government involved some very complex franchises. But by 1900 the position had been much simplified, and the local electorate of the occupiers of rateable property included about 75 per cent of all adult males and a few hundred thousand women. More people thus participated in local than in national elections. Whereas women were denied the vote in national elections, they had at least a toe-hold in local government. Women with sufficient property qualifications had been allowed to vote under the Municipal Franchise Act of 1869, though a court ruled a few years later that only unmarried women were so eligible. Women had been elected to school boards from 1870, and a woman was elected to be a Poor Law guardian in 1875, a position soon contested successfully by other women, so that in 1900 there were over 1,000 female guardians. Two women were elected to the LCC in 1889, though only in 1907 did a law specifically allow women to stand for election to county and borough councils and to become chairman or mayor (a position achieved first by Elizabeth Garrett Anderson the following year).

e) Professionalism

Local councils became more democratic as the century wore on, but councillors were still unpaid amateurs, despite the fact that their work became more and more complex. All the more important, therefore, was the work of the professionals, the paid local government officials. Local government became steadily more bureaucratic, as well as more democratic, after 1832. Whereas in 1851 there were 11,000 local government employees, not counting police, 30 years later this figure had risen to 51,000. Although the elected councillors, aldermen and mayors received the publicity, the town clerks, treasurers and other officials were the backbone of local government.

f) Overall Judgements

Should the word 'revolutionary' be used to describe the changes in the composition and duties of local government bodies that occurred in the nineteenth century? Many have judged that the growth that occurred was too slow and piecemeal for the term to be apt. But there can be no doubt that a fundamental reorganisation took place or that those affected by local services sometimes saw revolutionary changes in their lives.

The record of nineteenth century local government has been variously interpreted, as both success and failure. It depends very much on the position from which these judgements are made. To some there was an almost criminal neglect of preventable evils, especially in the realms of public health and housing, desolating the lives of many hundreds of thousands. To others, Britain's local institutions grappled, with ultimate success, against formidable problems that had never before been encountered, let alone solved, anywhere else in the world. Given the sheer variety of local institutions, which approached their work with different levels of energy and effectiveness, it would be a foolish historian who rushed in with any blanket generalisation other than the one which is perennially applicable to local government – that it comprises an enormous and contrasting area on which further research is needed.

Working on Chapter 5

Pay particular attention to the structure of local government institutions. This is a very complicated area, and therefore one which needs great care. As you cover each of the reforms, from 1835 to 1894, note how the basic structure of the local government system was changed. But do not allow concern for the form of local government to detract too much attention from the importance of the work that the different units of local government performed.

Summary Diagram
Local Government

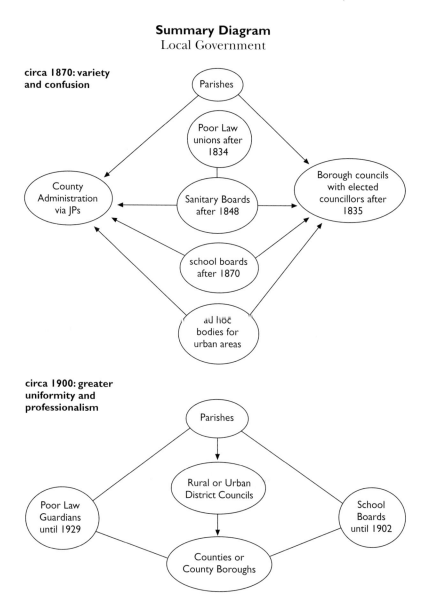

circa 1870: variety and confusion

Parishes

Poor Law unions after 1834

County Administration via JPs

Sanitary Boards after 1848

Borough councils with elected councillors after 1835

school boards after 1870

ad hoc bodies for urban areas

circa 1900: greater uniformity and professionalism

Parishes

Rural or Urban District Councils

Poor Law Guardians until 1929

School Boards until 1902

Counties or County Boroughs

Answering essay questions on Chapter 5

You will need some knowledge of local government to answer general questions on the growth of democracy, or of representative institutions, in nineteenth-century Britain. All too often students ignore this vital aspect and focus exclusively on parliament, thus losing marks simply for the want of a paragraph or two on local government. However, there are also questions specifically on the growth of local government institutions. The following are typical:

1. Assess the degree to which the Municipal Corporations Act of 1835 was both necessary and effective.
2. Why, and to what extent, did the aristocrats' control in the countryside diminish in the nineteenth century?
3. To what extent had a coherent and effective form of local administration been evolved in Britain by 1900?

Try to construct essay plans for each of these titles. It is always best to avoid straightforward narrative, and therefore you should give careful thought about how to begin the essays. If, for question 1, you start by giving a general statement about the terms of the 1835 Act, you could then look back, assessing the reasons for the legislation and whether it was necessary, and then look forward, assessing its impact and whether it was effective. Similarly, for question 2, you might begin by highlighting the 1888 Local Government Act as a landmark in the diminution of landowners' control of the countryside; then you could explain how and why this came about; and finally you could assess the extent to which landowners still had important powers and whether these amounted to 'control'.

Source-based questions on Chapter 5

1. R.W. Dale and Sidney Webb on local government
Read the extracts from Dale and Webb on pages 97 and 99, and answer the following questions:

a) Why did Dale believe the poor would benefit from 'parks and gardens … libraries and galleries of art' (lines 3–4)? (*2 marks*)
b) What else did Dale wish to see local government do, besides improve homes and public amenities? (*3 marks*)
c) What did Webb mean by the term 'individualist town councillor' (line 1)? (*2 marks*)
d) Basing your answer on both the tone and the content of the extract, explain Webb's attitude towards municipal trading. (*7 marks*)
e) Webb was writing 15 years after Dale. In what ways do their words reflect the changes that had occurred in local government over that time? (*11 marks*)

6 The Changing Role of the Monarchy

POINTS TO CONSIDER

During a period when the electoral system in particular and politics in general were undergoing profound changes, Britain's monarchy showed remarkably stability. You need to be aware of the ways in which the monarchy did change and of the reasons why change was not more extreme.

KEY DATES

1820–30	Reign of George IV: unpopularity.
1830–37	Reign of William IV: unpopularity.
1837	Accession of Queen Victoria: thereafter fluctuating popularity.
1840	Victoria married Prince Albert of Saxe-Coburg-Gotha.
1861	Death of Prince Albert from typhoid.
1864–83	John Brown's attendance on Victoria.
1871	Dilke's republican speech; illness of the Prince of Wales.
1873	Dilke's motion on the civil list defeated, 276 notes to 2.
1876	Queen Victoria made Empress of India.
1887	Golden Jubilee.
1897	Diamond Jubilee.
1901	Death of Victoria, accession of Edward VII.
1910	Death of Edward, accession of George V.

1 The Monarchy in 1837

KEY ISSUE What was the state of the monarchy at the time of Victoria's coronation?

In 1837, when Queen Victoria ascended the throne at the age of 17, the prestige and popularity of the British monarchy were at such a low ebb that some doubted that the institution would survive. The fault lay not with the new queen but with her predecessors.

George III (who reigned from 1760 to 1820) had died a lunatic and was succeeded by two sons, both of whom were disreputable characters. George IV (1820–30) was a dissolute and decadent personality. *The Times* wrote on his death that 'There never was an individual less regretted by his fellow-creatures than this deceased King. What eye wept for him? What heart has heaved one sob of unmercenary sorrow?' It averred that such an 'inveterate voluptuary', such an embodiment of selfishness, had surely never won a genuine friend in all his life. Yet even this strong language was mild compared with the personal comments of those who knew him well. One politician complained that 'a more contemptible, cowardly, selfish, unfeeling dog, does not exist than this king'. He was a well known womaniser, adulterer and indeed bigamist. He had married Caroline of Brunswick – herself a coarse and vulgar individual known at court as 'a fashionable strumpet' – conveniently disregarding a previous marriage.

George's brother, who reigned as William IV (1830–37), was, of necessity, something of an improvement. He was much more genial and accessible, but there was little else to be said in his favour. People described him as one part blackguard and three parts buffoon. According to the press, he was 'a weak, ignorant, commonplace sort of person', who suffered from 'feebleness of purpose and littleness of mind'. Another critic wrote scathingly of his 'numerous progeny of bastards'. Both brothers were condemned for squandering public money, and indeed in 1837 the Crown had large debts.

At Victoria's coronation *The Times* drew a distinction between the person of the monarch and the monarchy as an institution, insisting that the public's loyalty was to the latter. The people, it decreed, would preserve the monarchy with the help of their sovereign, if possible, but if necessary 'in spite of an ill-advised monarch'. Such a statement was a sign that monarchists were on the defensive, almost an admission that the worst enemies of kingship had been the previous kings. An impersonal institution could not suffer from human defects, whereas George III's offspring had been all too human. Yet the difference between the institution and the person was not an easy one for most people to maintain, especially since the trappings of monarchy in the early nineteenth century were tawdry in the extreme.

Royal rituals around this time, it has been said, 'oscillated between farce and fiasco'. At the funeral of a royal princess in 1817 the undertaker was drunk and at another, ten years later, Windsor Chapel was so cold that most of the mourners caught a chill and the Bishop of London subsequently died. At George IV's coronation prize-fighters had to be employed to keep order among the guests and at his funeral, one journalist noted, 'We never saw so motley, so rude, so ill-managed a body of persons'. William IV talked through the service and walked out early. Nor had things improved by 1837. At Victoria's coronation the clergy lost their place in the service, the choir was poor, the ring was too small for the new queen's finger, and two train-bearers talked throughout the ceremony. It was dubbed by one journal 'the shabby coronation'. Foreigners seemed to have a gift for dignified ceremonies, but not the British. Indeed Britons seemed almost proud of being bad at ceremonials: Britain was the workshop of the world not a fairground, and its people were pioneers of progress with no time for ritualistic fripperies. As a result, the British monarchy seemed to have no splendour or majesty, no magical associations. There was no 'divinity' hedging the monarch, as there had

'A voluptuary under the horrors of digestion', cartoon by Gillray.

been in Shakespeare's day. It was all too clear that, without the clothes of fine ritual, the emperor was naked. Cartoonists could therefore find regular royal targets for their satires, as with Gillray's caricature of George IV as Prince of Wales (see the cartoon above).

2 The Monarchical Paradox

> **KEY ISSUE** What explanations are there for the monarchy's survival during a period of democratisation?

Around 1837 many people judged that the monarchy was in danger of becoming a total laughing-stock. Furthermore, the extension of the franchise during the nineteenth century, beginning in 1832, seemed likely to undermine monarchical sentiment still further and add another to the growing list of Europe's republics. It was widely assumed that, with the growth of representative government, hereditary institutions like the monarchy and the House of Lords would wither away. In 1870 Prime Minister Gladstone did not see how the monarchy could survive for more than 30–40 years and in 1871 another leading politician of the day, Joseph Chamberlain, wrote that a republic would come 'in our generation'.

Yet the monarchy, by the end of the century, was flourishing. How do we account for the paradox of, on the one hand, increasing democratisation in British politics, and, on the other, the retention of the hereditary monarchy and its increased popularity? How was it that the monarchy managed to survive?

Perhaps the answer lies in the personality of the monarch. Whereas the monarchy survived in the first third of the nineteenth century in spite of the monarchs, did it flourish in the remainder because of Victoria herself? Or could it be that Victoria was 'packaged' so much more effectively than her predecessors, with elaborate and successful ceremony? But we also need to ask in what ways the Crown changed between the 1830s and the beginning of the twentieth century and in particular how its political functions evolved. Most historians have seen important connections between survival and evolution, between the social popularity of the monarchy and its decline in political importance. Did the monarchy swap power for popularity?

a) Diminished Unpopularity, 1837–61

The image conjured up in most people's minds of Queen Victoria is of an elderly, rather fat and unsmiling figure who was never amused but who was nevertheless immensely popular with her subjects. But it is important to remember that Queen Victoria's reign was the longest in British history and that during her 64 years on the throne she played many parts. At first, naturally enough, she was considered a breath of fresh air after her 'wicked uncles', George IV and William IV. In contrast to them, she was neither depraved nor corrupt, and she was a graceful and attractive figure. But it would be wrong to think that she was genuinely popular at this time. There were some, believing that no woman could adequately occupy the throne, who supported rival male claimants. Certainly her marriage to Albert of Saxe-Coburg in 1840 was decidedly unpopular. Albert was intelligent and industrious, a devoted family man, a good administrator and a discriminating patron of the arts, and the queen was quite devoted to him. But aristocrats disliked the atmosphere of dull respectability that surrounded the royal couple and found Albert too middle-class, unfashionably favouring chess rather than horse racing and even given to concern with the social conditions of the masses. To most people, he was simply a foreigner, a German prince, and thus immediately suspect. It was said that he had married Victoria for her money. One versifier insisted that Albert

> comes to take 'for better or worse'
> England's fat queen and England's fatter purse.

Such sentiments were unkind and unflattering. But there can be no doubt that over the next few years Victoria's figure did begin to spread: one who knew her well decided that 'she is more like a barrel than anything else'. Prince Albert was also far richer in England than he had been in Germany. The costs of the royal household also increased substantially after 1840, as a total of nine children were born to the royal couple. One royal birth in the 1840s was described by the *Northern Star*, a Chartist newspaper, as 'the birth of another royal tax-eater'. Critics drew attention to the fact that the central government's total spending on national education was smaller than that given, in the same year, to the royal stables, and charges of monarchical overspending were regularly levelled. Another common complaint was that Albert – who was given the title Prince Consort in 1857 – was trying to amass more power for the monarchy than the constitution legitimately allowed.

b) Increased Unpopularity, 1861–71

In 1861 Prince Albert died from typhoid. His death removed one cause of monarchical unpopularity (namely himself) but added another and greater one. Victoria went into deep and, it almost seemed, permanent mourning. She was, in her own words, an 'utterly brokenhearted and crushed widow of forty-two ... It is like losing half of one's body and soul, torn forcibly away'. Time scarcely seemed to heal the wound. She kept Albert's apartments exactly as they had been during his life and insisted that every evening his dress suit be laid out on his bed. 40 years after his death she confided to her journal that still she listened 'in the hope that he may yet come in, his door may open and his angelic form will return. I could go mad from the desire and longing!' Many thought she had. Certainly she never fully recovered from the death of her husband. She still worked hard at state business but lost all taste for public appearances. Her absence from royal occasions had been marked before the death of her husband, due to a state of almost permanent pregnancy, but now it threatened to become total. Her first public appearance, after the death, was not until June 1864, and they were infrequent thereafter. Usually she was away from London, most often at Balmoral Castle in Scotland or Osborne in the Isle of Wight. (One wit even pinned a 'For Sale' notice to the railings of Buckingham Palace.) She would not entertain foreign visitors and rarely would she agree to preside at the opening of parliament. She insisted that poor health would not allow her to undertake such duties. Yet she regularly applied to parliament for marriage or coming-of-age grants for her children, and many believed her guilty of malingering. Certainly her virtual disappearance seemed to confirm to a growing number of critics that Britain could get along quite nicely without a monarch. After all, asserted the radical journalist and politician Charles Bradlaugh, it was already doing so.

Rumours about the queen multiplied rapidly. Some said that, like her grandfather, she had gone mad. Others, with a taste for scandal, believed that she was having an affair with a serving man, the Scotsman John Brown, with whom she had become infatuated. A popular nickname for Victoria became 'Mrs Brown', and there were rumours that she had borne a child during one of her long absences from the public gaze. Historians still debate the truth of such charges. There was certainly a good deal of familiarity and affection between the queen and her favourite servant, much to the chagrin of Victoria's children. She wrote to him as 'my best friend' and 'darling one', and at her death she chose to be buried not only with Albert's dressing gown but also with a photograph and some hair of Brown. But the most significant aspect of this issue is not whether the rumours were true or not but that they were regularly repeated and widely believed: they are a reflection of the low ebb of monarchical fortunes in the 1860s. Here was further grist to the mill of political satirists. (See the cartoon, 'A Brown Study', below, in which John Brown leans against

'A Brown Study', cartoon from *The Tomahawk*, August 1867.

an empty throne, regardless of the British lion.) There were calls for Victoria to abdicate in favour of her eldest son, Edward the Prince of Wales, though not everyone believed the Prince would be an improvement. Victoria herself had a low opinion of 'Bertie'. He had been the subject of a scandal with an actress during his father's last illness and was cited as a co-respondent in a divorce case in 1870. 'To speak in rude and general terms,' wrote Gladstone towards the end of this year, 'the Queen is invisible, and the Prince of Wales is not respected'.

c) The Climax of Republicanism

Not surprisingly, republicanism grew in this period. It was boosted by events elsewhere, especially in France where the Third Republic was proclaimed in 1870. It was also fed by royal rumour and scandal and drew sustenance from the cost to the nation of the royal family. Republicanism in Britain reached its peak in 1870–1, a period of unemployment and some social discontent. The constitutional expert Walter Bagehot, writing in *The Economist*, argued that Victoria, by her long retirement from public life, had done almost as much to injure the popularity of the monarchy 'as the most unworthy of her predecessors did by his profligacy and frivolity'. An anonymous pamphlet of this time, *What does she do with it?*, accused the queen of hoarding around £200,000 a year. Several large anti-monarchical demonstrations were held in London towards the end of 1870, and early the following year over 50 republican clubs were set up in Britain's major cities. Also in 1871 Bradlaugh published *The Impeachment of the House of Brunswick*, attacking the first four Georges and urging that the monarchy be abolished on Victoria's death. In the House of Commons over 60 Members voted either to reduce or refuse altogether an allowance for one of the royal children. The climax came in November 1871, when the most prominent of these MPs, Sir Charles Dilke, the radical member for Chelsea, came out in favour of the republican principle in a rally held at Newcastle.

In a speech to a working-class audience which was greeted with great enthusiasm, Dilke insisted that the Crown was burdensomely expensive and produced inefficiency in public life:

1 I think that, speaking roughly, you may say that the positive and direct cost of the Royalty is about a million a year. In addition ... it is worth remembering that the Royal Family pay no taxes ... In ... the Army, we have a Royal Duke, not necessarily the fittest man, at the head of it by
5 right of birth, and the Prince of Wales, who would never be allowed a command in time of war, put to lead the Cavalry Divisions in the Autumn Manoeuvres (laughter), thus robbing working officers of the position and of the training they had a title to expect. ('Hear' and great applause.) Now, institutions are not good or bad in themselves, so
10 much as good or bad by their working, and we are told that a limited Monarchy works well. I set aside, in this speech, the question of

whether a Republic would work better; but I confess freely that I doubt whether ... the monarchy should not set its house in order. (Loud applause.) There is a widespread belief that a Republic here is only a
20 matter of time. (Great cheering.) It is said that some day a Commonwealth will be our Government. Now, history and experience show that you cannot have a Republic without you possessing at the same time the Republican virtues. But you answer – Have we not the public spirit? Have we not the practice of self-government? Are we not
25 gaining general education? (Applause.) Well, if you can show me a fair chance that a republic will be free from the general corruption which hangs about the Monarchy, I say, for my part – and I believe that the middle classes will say – let it come. (Cheers.)

After reading the speech, Victoria was reported as 'crying a lot and being regularly unhappy'. But she had many defenders, not least *The Times*:

1 Now we pass over the presumption which emboldens Sir Charles Dilke to speak in the name of the middle classes, and forbear to enquire how far he may be himself indebted to Royal favour. Looking only at the language as it is reported, and remembering that it comes from a member
5 of the Legislature, we cannot but recognise it as a recklessness bordering on criminality. Sir Charles 'sets aside the question whether a Republic would not work better,' as if this were not the whole question to be decided, and as if anything could justify the attempt to excite the working class audience against their existing Government, except a firm
10 conviction, supported by solid proofs, that it could be replaced by something better ... Sir Charles is prospectively willing to risk the destruction of a Monarchy at least a thousand years old, though he defers till a more convenient season any statement of the little plan which he may have for a new Constitution ... But even these [alle-
15 gations of waste and nepotism] are not fair and legitimate points ... to be handled, and that with little candour or delicacy, before an assembly of working men ...

Other monarchists, with less delicacy, asserted that Dilke should be shot.

From Newcastle, Dilke moved on to other venues. At Bolton bricks were thrown through the window of the hall where he spoke and one republican was killed. Back in London he was socially ostracised, finding himself with scarcely a friend, and when in March 1873 he introduced a motion in the Commons calling for an enquiry into the Civil List he was given a very hostile reception. As for the motion, it was defeated by 276 votes to 2. Not surprisingly, therefore, at the general election of 1874 Dilke insisted that he was not a republican candidate and that, at Newcastle, nothing had been further from his mind than to impute blame to Her Majesty: he was heartily sorry that his words were understood in this sense and 'the very fact that they were shows that they were wrong'. Such penitence reveals that the republican tide had run its course.

d) Monarchy Triumphant, 1871–1901

The resurrection of monarchical fortunes was partly fortuitous. The climax of republicanism occurred just as illness brought about a wave of popular sympathy – what one newspaper called a 'great epidemic of typhoid loyalty' – for the monarchy. A few days after the Newcastle speech, the Prince of Wales fell ill. He seemed likely to die ten years after his father, and of the same illness. Hope had almost been abandoned when recovery set in, to a wave of public rejoicing. When, in February 1872, the queen and the prince drove to a national thanksgiving service in St Paul's Cathedral, there were scenes of tremendous enthusiasm such as no royalist could remember. The mood was kept alive when, the very next day, an unsuccessful – and half-hearted – attempt was made on the queen's life.

Yet the monarchical triumph also owed much to design, to the Victorian equivalent of modern-day public relations experts. The monarchy began to be presented as a glorious national institution and a focus for splendid pageantry. In short, the monarchy harnessed feelings of nationalism at a time, following the unification of Germany in 1871, when imperial rivalry between the Great Powers was beginning to dominate the European continent. The monarchy became a symbol of British national and imperial greatness. Patriotism was harnessed by the monarchy. In a similar way, the monarchy was harnessed by the Conservative party. Indeed to a large extent the new image of the monarchy was devised by Benjamin Disraeli, who became Conservative prime minister in 1874 and who wished to associate his party with monarchical and patriotic sentiment in order to win the votes of the newly enfranchised electors.

Victoria heartily disliked his great rival, the Liberal leader William Gladstone, but she had a soft spot for 'Dizzy'. Indeed she even allowed him to sit down in her presence, an honour she had accorded to none of her premiers since her first, Lord Melbourne. 'Gladstone treats the Queen like a public department,' explained Disraeli; 'I treat her like a woman.' But the fullest explanation of his success was given just before his death. 'Everyone likes flattery,' he told a friend, 'and when you come to royalty, you should lay it on with a trowel.' A rather flirtatious relationship grew up between the queen and the Tory leader, to the satisfaction of them both. In 1876 Disraeli's government, at the queen's request, made Victoria Empress of India, and so the British monarchy became an imperial institution, symbolising the new imperial sentiment that was over the next two decades to accompany the expansion of the British empire. In many ways this was a masterstroke, generating new popularity for the monarchy.

As an Empress, Victoria would not be outshone by the Emperors of

Germany, Austria-Hungary or Russia. The British monarchy would be no one's poor relation. Hence royal ritual was vastly improved, and the British even began fondly to imagine that they had always been adept at such ceremonial splendour. The established church now began to take ritual seriously. Westminster Abbey was given a face-lift: its organ was rebuilt, the choir was given red cassocks and a new cross was provided for the high altar. Music was taken very seriously, aided by composers like Parry and Elgar ('the nation's unofficial music laureate'). Similarly the capital city was made grander. New splendid buildings were erected, monuments proliferated and Buckingham Palace was re-fronted. The British monarchy would outdo its rivals, partly by a new splendour, partly by preserving its heritage: royal coaches, made anachronistic by developments in motor transport, would invest the royal progress through the streets of London with popular appeal. No longer were royal rituals poorly performed behind closed doors; they were staged (and stage-managed) with great success as national spectacles. Victoria was still reluctant to appear on ceremonial occasions, but each one was now given a blaze of publicity. Indeed it was hard for the public to avoid her image – in newspapers, due to new photographic techniques, on the coinage, on stamps, on commemorative pottery and medals, and even on advertisements by firms such as Rowntree, Cadbury and Oxo.

It was all illusion, but successful illusion. Victoria was transformed from a neurotic old woman into the 'faery queen'. She was not merely head of state but the leader and symbol of the nation and its greatness – the mother of her people. Her popularity, seen in the celebrations for the Golden Jubilee in 1887 and especially for the Diamond Jubilee of 1897, was unmistakable. Victoria did not like all the pomp and ceremony of these occasions, and she resolutely refused to wear the crown and robes of state, but she found the enthusiasm of the massive crowds 'truly marvellous and deeply touching. The cheering was quite deafening, and every face seemed to be filled with real joy.'

The socialist Keir Hardie tried to laugh off the jubilees as 'bread and circuses without the bread'. But the cheering crowds were swept along in a cavalcade of pageantry. Indeed the Diamond Jubilee was the 'apotheosis' of monarchy: Victoria, a woman with her fair share of human faults, had been transformed almost into a goddess. In the words of one historian, she was 'more an icon and symbol than a real human being.' No wonder *The Times*, at her death, was able to comment that the popularity of the monarchy was due in large measure to Victoria herself – 'to the womanly sweetness, the gentle sagacity, the utter disinterestedness, and the unassailable rectitude of the Queen'. It is of such stuff that myths are made.

e) Victoria's Successors

The Prince of Wales became king as Edward VII in 1901. In his earlier years he had been the subject of much scandal, and his private life was certainly not above reproach. Many have described him as an incredible glutton. Kipling described him as 'a corpulent voluptuary of no importance', and a popular nickname among those who knew him well was 'Tum-tum'. Edward disliked hard work and generally spent three months of every year abroad. But monarchy at this period had little to do with real human beings: it was a matter of image and illusion. Fortunately, the new king loved dressing up, took a positive delight in ceremony and revelled in pageantry, and indeed he revived the state opening of Parliament as a major state occasion. Hence it was not difficult to pass him off as a dignified, indeed glorious, figurehead.

George V, who became king in 1910, was an even less promising subject for adulation. His biographer has written that 'For seventeen years he did nothing at all but kill animals and stick in stamps.' But no matter. He was presented as the perfect family man (despite the fact that to his own children he was harsh and unreasonable), a figure of tolerance and inspired common sense (regardless of his habit of swearing at servants and his inability to smile) and a reassuring symbol of stability in a world of disconcerting change. It was said that when he died in 1936, 'the sunset of his death tinged the whole world's sky'. The image-makers, supported by a sycophantic press, had been successfully at work. They were helped enormously by the fact that new sources of monarchical propaganda were at their disposal, including the radio, on which George V began regular Christmas broadcasts, and newsreels, which conveyed the spectacle of royal rituals to more people than ever before.

3 The Powers of the Monarchy

> **KEY ISSUE** Did the monarchy swap power for popularity?

At the end of the 1860s the constitutional theorist Walter Bagehot wrote of the monarchy that 'mystery is its life' and urged that daylight should not be allowed to disturb its magic. He judged that the monarchy belonged to the 'dignified' part of the constitution, more ornamental than useful, the monarch having but three rights, 'the right to be consulted, the right to encourage, the right to warn'. In this classic statement, Bagehot argued that the Crown had, in effect, swapped real political power for symbolic, magical associations. It had survived, therefore, not only by becoming associated with ceremony and pageantry but by abandoning political power. Yet we should not be tempted to accept this view too readily. After all, when Bagehot was writing the Crown had not yet become associated with fine ritual: in the 1860s the monarchy was still relatively unpopular and royal ritual was remarkably inept. The other problem with his interpretation arises from the fact that neither the queen nor her ministers read constitutional textbooks. No one had told them that royal powers were so limited. Indeed so tenacious was Victoria in trying to get her own way that Gladstone once cried out in despair that 'The Queen is enough to kill a man'.

The truth of the matter is that Bagehot, like most other commentators, described what he believed ought to be, rather than what actually was, the case. Since the British constitution was not written down as a single document, or set of documents, it was, to a large degree, a matter of conventions, traditions and political habits. One jurist called it a 'bundle of usages'. It did not effectively define the limits of monarchical power. In other words, the constitution was often a subject of fierce debate in the nineteenth century, and conceptions of legitimate practice were continually evolving. The constitution, in fact, is perhaps best seen as the sum total of what actually happened. Hence as historians we can only trace the shifting pattern of what monarchs were able to do.

As for centuries past, each British law required the consent of the monarch, the Commons and the Lords. Parliament was thus a trinity of powers, but the relationship between them was rarely static. The Crown also had certain 'prerogative' powers necessary to ensure the defence and good ordering of the realm, including the power to grant honours and make appointments, but these were poorly defined. It was an accepted convention by the beginning of the nineteenth century that government was carried on not by the monarch but by ministers in his or her name, but the division between what a monarch did on the advice of ministers and what he might do on his own was far from clear, leaving room for considerable strife between monarch and ministers.

a) The pre-1837 Era

Queen Anne (1702–14) had used her veto to disallow a bill passed by the Lords and the Commons. In fact she was the last monarch ever to use the royal veto; but for a long time it seemed quite possible that subsequent monarchs would also refuse to consent to bills. Certainly their theoretical power to do so was not removed, and in the eighteenth century monarchs were very important politically. It was the monarch who appointed the prime minister and, with his advice, all the other ministers, and only the king (or queen) could determine the exact timing of a general election. Furthermore, the Crown controlled a number of 'rotten boroughs' and the men – around 100 in 1800 – placed in them. George III was able to use his powers to keep ministers in office even when they had lost the support of the House of Commons, and in his seven-year reign William IV twice dissolved parliament before its time and three times dissolved ministries he disliked. In 1835 William insisted that no government could survive without the active support of the monarch. Certainly it was rarely possible to foist on a monarch either a prime minister or policies of which he disapproved.

Nevertheless, although in constitutional theory royal powers remained exactly the same, in practice royal authority definitely declined in the period from 1829 to 1832. In 1829 Prime Minister Wellington virtually gave an ultimatum to George IV over the controversial Catholic Emancipation bill (see page 35). The monarch shared to the full the prejudices of so many Protestants at this time in regarding Catholics as idolatrous, superstitious and somehow sinister and un-English. Nevertheless, the king accepted that henceforth Catholics should be allowed to become MPs. Even more significantly, a few years later William IV accepted the Great Reform Bill, going so far as to agree to use his prerogative to create enough peers to ensure its passage through the Lords (see page 43). Both George and William had declined to exercise their right to defy their ministers, and as a result such rights became even more theoretical than before. Furthermore, the newly 'reformed' parliamentary system saw the loss of royal 'placemen' in the Commons. Indeed, under this new political dispensation, it soon became accepted that the Crown would not interfere in any elections. Royal powers over the Commons therefore began to ebb.

b) Victoria's Reign

Royal powers had declined before Victoria came to the throne – so much so that a contemporary French monarch declared that he would rather chop wood than be King of England! Even so the young queen was not given to meekly accepting what her prime ministers decided. The first crisis came very early in her reign. In 1839 Lord Melbourne, whose majority in the Commons was very slender, decided to resign and give Peel a chance to form a government. But Victoria refused Peel's request that she should replace several ladies-in-waiting, who were relatives of Whig ministers. This was the 'bedchamber crisis', the upshot of which was that Melbourne stayed on as prime minister until 1841. Victoria's actions were dictated by two motives, a liking for Melbourne, whom she wished to retain as prime minister, and the belief that the government was *hers* and that therefore she would not be dictated to. She certainly did not consider that her role as monarch was politically neutral and that she was merely an ornamental figurehead. She was politically partisan and remained actively so for the rest of her life.

Victoria did not develop her views into any political theory. Instead she reacted instinctively to political events. But Prince Albert was much more a theorist. His views, strongly influenced by practice elsewhere in Europe, included the idea that the monarch was the 'natural guardian of the honour of his country' and that therefore he had of necessity to be a politician. He would loyally accept as prime minister whoever could command a majority in the Commons, but he would not tamely accept whatever policies the government of the day decided. Yet Albert's trail was not followed. His systematic views would have probably enhanced the political powers of the monarch, and might have produced a republican backlash. As it was, the British muddled along their trackless path.

After Albert's death, Victoria much preferred Disraeli to Gladstone. She was far happier and readier to appoint the former as prime minister, but the choice was not always hers. In 1880, despite huffing and puffing ('she would sooner abdicate than send for ... that half-mad fire-brand who would soon ruin everything and be a Dictator'), she had to acquiesce in the choice of Gladstone, and two years later she even had to endorse the choice of Sir Charles Dilke, whose republican speech had so upset her less than a decade earlier, as a cabinet minister. Similarly, while insisting on being consulted and on giving her opinion on government policies, and especially on foreign policy, she did not always get her way. She was unsympathetic towards the extension of the franchise which successive governments brought about and towards the factory legislation fostered by both Liberals and Tories. Had Victoria's ideas been accepted, Britain would also have pursued a far more pro-Prussian foreign policy during Bismarck's wars of 1864–71.

On the other hand, Victoria was certainly no mere gilded rubber stamp. In 1851, protesting, quite correctly, that the Foreign Secretary, Lord Palmerston, had been sending off dispatches without allowing her to see them, she had Palmerston dismissed. She also maintained a lengthy correspondence on foreign affairs with her European relatives, and often managed to persuade ministers to send her information about cabinet meetings to supplement the descriptions sent by her premiers. She insisted on having an important say in the choice of officers for the army's high command and she took her position as 'supreme head' of the Church of England very seriously, insisting on getting her nominee chosen as Archbishop of Canterbury in 1868.

There was no conscious decision on Victoria's part that the Crown should be less politically powerful, and certainly there was no simple, linear pattern of decline of political influence for the monarchy in Victoria's reign. In 1852 it was she and she alone who decided that Lord Aberdeen should become Prime Minister, and in 1894 Lord Rosebery was her personal choice as premier. Nevertheless there was a broad pattern of political decline for the Victorian monarchy. This can be explained by several factors, including the queen's declining powers in her last years. But above all it is a reflection of the growth of parties in the House of Commons. In the words of one expert: 'The King rose above politics only when the parties pushed him there.' The monarch's political power varied in inverse proportion to the political power of the largest party in the Commons. When the party system was fluid and governments had to be coalitions dependent on the shifting alignments of factions at Westminster, the monarch was at her most powerful and influential. This was very much the situation at the start of Victoria's reign and also in 1851–9 . But when governments were stable, enjoying a safe majority of seats and led by a clearly chosen figure, the monarch's powers were immediately curtailed. This was certainly the case in 1880 when Victoria had to acquiesce not only in Gladstone's appointment as Prime Minister but also in his policies, many of which were anathema to her. She threatened to dissolve parliament if certain bills were accepted by Commons and Lords, but in the end she had to content herself, in the words of one historian, with trying to nag Gladstone to death.

c) Edward VII and George V

After Victoria's death there was no resurrection of monarchical political power, not least because the parties at Westminster became ever more effective political machines. In sharp contrast to a century earlier, the monarch now had little say in the choice of prime minister: except in very exceptional circumstances, he merely rubber-stamped the verdict of the electorate and the House of Commons. Nor did Edward VII, or from 1910 George V, really work hard enough to challenge the professional politicians. They were figureheads far more than Victoria had ever been. It has been said that George V was the first king really to fit Bagehot's description of a king, politically neutral and claiming the right merely to be consulted, to encourage and to warn. The crisis between Commons and Lords in 1909–12 (see chapter 8) showed that real power lay with the elected representatives of the people, in that the monarch was willing, in the end, to create hundreds of new peers to ensure the dominance of the elected government of the day.

Nevertheless, George V took his duties seriously. In 1914 the Liberal government was about to pass a law to give Home Rule to Ireland, a measure of which Queen Victoria had heartily disapproved and which was also anathema to her grandson. George V warned the prime minister that he would 'feel it his duty to do what in his own judgement was best for the people generally'. Almost certainly he was considering the use of the royal veto, even at the expense of a full-scale constitutional crisis. The fact that he even considered doing so shows that the course of political decline for the monarchy had not run totally smoothly.

4 Conclusion

KEY ISSUE Why did the monarchy survive?

The nineteenth century had been an age of growing democratisation, even though universal suffrage did not arrive until after the First World War. How was it, then, that an hereditary monarchy managed not only to survive but to grow more popular? First it must be recognised that though Britain became more democratic as the nineteenth century wore on, it remained a society of deep social and economic inequalities. The existence of an hereditary monarchy would have been unthinkable in a truly classless society. As it was, the continued existence of the monarchy may be seen as reflecting the concentrations of wealth and power that existed even in democratising Britain.

Next it should be pointed out that the monarchy's chances of survival were much greater because fully representative government arrived slowly and incrementally. If democracy had been introduced at a stroke, the monarchy's position would have seemed glaringly anomalous. Equally important is the fact that the monarchy evolved during these important years: its theoretical position in the British constitution did not change, but in practice its powers declined. Indeed, it can even be argued that the monarchy did not survive. A French observer noted in the reign of Edward VII that 'England is in reality a republic wearing the semblance and invested with the forms of a monarchy.' The old monarchy, as it existed in 1800, was not to be found in Britain in 1900. It had perished as surely as Old Sarum. A new monarchy had taken its place, with less political power but with a dignity enhanced by rejuvenated royal ritual and effective royal propaganda. By a stroke of public relations genius, the monarchy had been reinterpreted: it was not a bizarre, anachronistic survival but a vital symbol of British national and imperial might.

The importance of this new 'packaging' of the monarchy must be stressed. The socialist Keir Hardie had thought that the greater exposure of royalty to the public gaze would demystify monarchy and be its undoing. A fraud, he insisted, should be shrouded from the popular gaze, and therefore 'Royalty to be a success should keep off the streets.' No doubt Hardie was correct, in a sense. Had members of the public seen the reality of the royal family, they would surely have recognised them as merely human. But instead they were presented with glamorous and highly idealised images of Victoria and her family, romantically and nationalistically charged. It was safe for royalty to travel the streets – but only in a gilded carriage.

Victoria had certainly not wanted nor expected these developments: she had a contempt for democracy and was always conscious of her own dignity. But she had certainly played her part in them, not least by always loyally supporting whichever prime minister parliamentary politics threw her way, with the partial exception of Gladstone. Above all, she had not effectively challenged the direction of political evolution, avoiding head-on collision with the forces of democracy. She did not allow the monarchy to become a major obstacle to reform – wisely, for sometimes major obstacles have to be removed. As a result, the process of 'modernisation' could proceed under Britain's constitutional monarchy. (Some credit should also go to the 'wicked uncles'. By accepting Catholic Emancipation and the Great Reform Bill, in 1829 and 1832, they had boosted the idea that change could be achieved peacefully, with royal approval.) But it was due to Victoria, not her predecessors, that the monarchy was given a new legitimacy which bridged the gap between old-fashioned notions of hereditary power and the newer notions of representative government. As *The Times* noted, at her death, the monarchy was 'broad-based upon the people's will'. A popular government necessitated either a republic, with an elected head of state, or a popular monarchy. Britain had the latter, and only a minority of critics complained.

It is also important to examine the anti-monarchical forces in Britain. After all, Britain *was* a monarchy, and therefore the onus was on those who would remove it. But in fact republicans were unequal to the task and never posed an effective challenge to the monarchy. Early on, the radicals had been over-confident that the monarchy would fall: Tom Paine, for instance, had predicted in the 1790s that it had only another seven years' life. Their views almost formed a self-defeating prophecy. So obvious did it seem to them that monarchy must collapse, as governments became responsive to people's wishes, that few radicals saw the need to take any action actually to bring about a republic. Instead, their energies went into campaigning for an extension of the franchise – an exhausting campaign that was not in fact complete until well into the twentieth century. Later republicans, like Dilke, were cautious in their actions, theorists rather than active campaigners. Yet to most members of the British public, republicanism always seemed somehow not quite respectable: it was associated with disreputable people like Dilke, whose involvement in a divorce case in 1886 caused him temporarily to leave public life, or like Charles Bradlaugh, infamous as an atheist and believer in birth control. Indeed to oppose the monarchy seemed disloyal and unpatriotic. Most people almost automatically supported the monarchy, so great and so successful was the anti-republican movement after 1871.

There are many other, miscellaneous reasons for the survival of the monarchy. Luck played its part, with the almost providential illness of the Prince of Wales in 1871, a time when the sorely-pressed monarchy was in great need of popular sympathy. Victoria's longevity was also important, age making her into something of a national institution. So was the fact that from the 1880s onwards the popular press and the state educational system encouraged conservative and deferential attitudes to the Crown. Continental republics, like France after 1870, were often seen as rivals rather than exemplars, and Britain seemed to be prospering under its constitutional monarchy. Was not Victorian England the most economically advanced country in the world? What was the point in altering a system which was doing so well? And when things did go wrong, it made much more sense to blame the politicians who formulated policy, rather than the monarchy which merely acquiesced in it. Many historians have speculated that had Britain lost the First World War, the British monarchy might well have toppled. The war saw the downfall of the Romanov, Hohenzollern and Habsburg dynasties (in Russia, Germany and Austria respectively). Who can tell whether the British royal family (which had changed its name from Saxe-Coburg-Gotha to the eminently English Windsor in 1917) might not have gone the same way? Yet these continental dynasties had had greater executive power in 1914 than the British. Having only a limited amount of political power, the British monarchy – while celebrating victories with lavish spectacle – could not be held responsible for failures.

The French king early in the nineteenth century who commented scathingly that he would rather chop wood than be King of England was in fact toppled from his throne in a revolution. Similarly the monarchs of 1914, who may have looked with disdain on their politically weaker British brethren, were in 1918 forced to abdicate, if they were not, like the Russian Romanovs, lying dead in a ditch. British monarchs had adapted to the forces of democracy to a degree they may have disliked, but at least they had survived.

Working on Chapter 6

Your notes should be constructed around the question 'Why did the monarchy survive?' This requires an understanding of (i) the state of the monarchy before Victoria's reign, (ii) the changing popularity of Victoria, (iii) the gradual decline in monarchical powers, and (iv) the republican movement. Finally, you should attempt to arrange the summary of factors in section 5 of this chapter into some sort of rank order of importance. Can you identify any extra causes of monarchical survival?

Summary Diagram
The Changing Role of the Monarchy

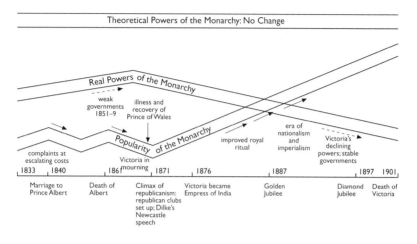

Most questions centre on the key issues of the monarchy's powers and popularity, together with its political survival. Here is a typical structured question:

I. a) What grievances did radicals have with the British monarchy, 1832–71? (*5 marks*)
b) In what ways did the monarchy improve its 'image' under Queen Victoria? (*5 marks*)
c) Account for the survival of the monarchy in Victorian England. (*10 marks*)

The first two parts of this question should present few difficulties for those who have read this chapter carefully. The third section, however, is more taxing. Be sure to built upon your answers to a) and b). The extra issues you will need to raise include the strength of the radicals and whether the powers of the monarchy changed.

Consider also the following essay titles:

1. In what ways and to what extent did the powers of the Crown diminish between 1837 and 1910?
2. Why was the British monarchy not abolished in the nineteenth century.

Construct plans for these titles. For the first title, you might stress in your opening paragraph the nature of the decline in the Crown's powers – the fact that powers fell into disuse rather than being formally abolished – and that powers might be resurrected to some extent when governments were weak. After your introductory paragraph, you could have paragraphs on particular powers. Probably most students would favour this sort of analytical structure, at least at first; but the individual 'powers' of the Crown were probably not as important as its overall strength, and therefore it is worthwhile considering a chronological framework, within which you could focus on 'ways' and 'extent'. Such a structure would enable you to answer the precise question set (and avoid the obvious pitfall of focusing, quite irrelevantly, on the reasons for the diminution of monarchical powers). For the final paragraph, you could make direct contrasts between 1837 and 1910.

The second question is relatively straightforward. It is in fact virtually the same as the final part of the structured question. The way to approach it is to think what smaller questions it is composed of. You will need more than two. Once you've formulated half a dozen subdivisions, pay special attention, to the order in which your points, which should each warrant a paragraph, appear in the plan. Can you devise a structure which will enable your paragraphs 'naturally' to succeed one another, each one logically connecting with the next?

Source-based questions on Chapter 6

1. Dilke and The Times on Republicanism

Read the extracts from Sir Charles Dilke's speech at Newcastle in 1871 and the comments from *The Times*, on pages 113 and 114, and answer the following questions:

a) Give two examples from the speech of 'the general corruption which hangs about the monarchy' (lines 22–3). (*4 marks*)
b) Was Dilke a Republican on principle? Explain your answer. (*2 marks*)
c) From the evidence contained in the speech, do you think that Dilke believed that a Republic might come about in the short term? (*3 marks*)
d) Was *The Times* justified in saying that, in Dilke's view, he spoke 'in the name of the middle classes' (line 2)? (*3 marks*)
e) Why do you think the newspaper forbore to enquire how far Dilke might be 'indebted to Royal favour' (line 3)? (*2 marks*)
f) Why do you think that *The Times* was so concerned that he was addressing a working-class audience? (*2 marks*)
g) Using your knowledge of the period, estimate the likely support that each side in this debate had in the country. (*9 marks*)

7 The Liberals, the Lords and Reform, 1906–14

POINTS TO CONSIDER

From 1906 to 1911 there was a crisis between the House of Commons and the House of Lords. You need to understand why confrontation occurred between them and the nature of the settlement that was reached in 1911. How far was the crisis caused by particular individuals, and how far by underlying, structural factors?

KEY DATES

1905	Liberal government took office under Campbell-Bannerman.
1906	general election: Liberal landslide.
1906–8	Lords veto Liberal bills.
1908	Asquith became prime minister, Lloyd George chancellor of the exchequer.
1909	(April) Lloyd George's 'People's Budget'; (Nov.) Lords rejected the budget.
1910	(Jan.) general election: narrow victory for Liberals; (May) death of Edward VII and accession of George V; (Dec.) second general election: tie between Liberals and Conservatives.
1911	(August) Lords accepted Parliament Bill.

1 The House of Lords around 1900

> **KEY ISSUE** Why was trouble brewing between Lords and Commons early in the twentieth century?

The tide of parliamentary reform, which so affected the Commons from 1832 onwards, left the House of Lords remarkably unscathed. The House of Commons had been substantially reformed by 1884–5, and it was recognised that its power was derived from the consent of a large section of the male population. Of course, the more democratic the House of Commons became, the more anachronistic the House of Lords seemed. Yet the Lords was not ashamed of being an hereditary chamber, representing the principle that Britain's 'natural' rulers were the members of its landowning elite. Their lordships took it for granted that the landowning class was also the governing class. Government – more than hunting, shooting or fishing – was the true sport of the nobility. The two Houses thus represented different theories of government – democracy (rule by the people) and aristocracy (rule by the nobility). Tension between them was surely only to be expected, and some believed that a head-on collision was virtually certain. Might there even be a fight to the death? The Upper House exhibited tenacious powers of survival in the nineteenth century. As one socialist writer complained, the aristocrats were made of 'curiously tough substance'. Between 1850 and 1880 hardly anyone questioned the nobility's superiority. 'We are', complained a radical in this period, 'a servile, aristocracy-loving, lord-ridden people'. The Lords' success stemmed partly from the fact that the Commons was for so long open to aristocratic influence. Indeed, until the 1880s, the Lower House was essentially a landowners' club. Only in 1885 did businessmen finally outnumber landed MPs, and a majority of every Cabinet until 1905 was composed of members of the British landed establishment. Similarly, most nineteenth-century prime ministers sat in the Lords rather than the Commons, Disraeli being the only head of government to have no landed connections. The Lords jealously guarded their parliamentary powers, and did so with success. Their theoretical constitutional position in 1900 was as it had been for centuries. Since the passage of any Bill into law required the agreement of Monarch, Lords and Commons, it followed that the Lords could veto any measure by withholding consent. Peers could be forgiven for thinking towards the end of the nineteenth century that they would continue to exercise political power well into the twentieth.

Yet pessimists in the Upper House could see the writing on the wall. A sombre background was created by the deteriorating economic position of landowners in Britain, which so affected their position in local administration. Of course there were still fantastically wealthy peers, and many wisely invested their wealth in industry; but, as a class, British landowners suffered greatly after 1880 from the fall in agricultural prices and rents that affected the whole of Europe. The decline of the aristocracy, described by one expert as 'a gradual long-drawn-out revolution', was undoubtedly well under way before the end of the nineteenth century in terms of both wealth and social status. There was also a decline in political influence, especially in the House of Commons. Legislation such as the Corrupt and Illegal Practices Act of 1883 made elections cheaper and more democratic, resulting in landed magnates 'controlling' fewer seats (see page 68). In addition, the growth of the electorate led to the formation of democratic parties and encouraged the view that political legitimacy derived solely from election. Those whose power depended on tradition were therefore thrown very much on to the defensive. Politics was also becoming more professional, leaving less scope for the lordly amateur. Even the House of Lords could not escape changes. Whereas earlier in the century new peerages had generally been bestowed on those from traditional landed families, from the 1880s they began to go to the *nouveaux riches*, those whose profits derived from industry rather than agriculture. In the period 1880–1914 200 new peerages were created, twice as many as in the same period before 1880. But only 25 per cent of these went to men from traditional landed families; the rest went to industrialists or those who had risen in the professions or public service. Some stigmatised the House of Lords, and its new brewery magnates, as quite simply a rich man's club.

a) The Vexatious Veto

During the nineteenth century the Lords still retained vitally important constitutional powers, but political convention and practice did change. It became accepted, for example, that only a vote of no confidence in the House of Commons could force a government to resign; a similar vote in the Lords would have no effect. It was also accepted that the Lords would not veto a 'money bill' (budget), since a refusal to vote supplies would paralyse government. In short, some sort of *modus vivendi* between the two Houses was worked out. Yet the Lords' capacity to veto legislation remained a real bone of contention. They had the constitutional capacity to amend or veto Bills put before them: but after the Third Reform Act they might well be overturning measures sanctioned by the people, or at least by a majority of adult men. Did they have the moral, as opposed to the legal, right to do this? The problem was compounded by the fact that from the 1880s onwards the House of Lords had a large Conservative majority. In 1886 the Liberal Party split over Irish Home Rule, and the 'Liberal Unionist' peers made common cause the Conservatives. A Conservative majority of 60–70 in 1868 had reached 400 by 1893.

The peers had opposed vital government measures before. The Great Reform Bill of 1832 had been accepted by the Upper House only after the king had promised, if necessary, to create enough new peers to ensure the Bill's success; and almost the same situation had occurred in 1884, when it was mooted that the veto should be removed from the Lords and a campaign had been launched to abolish the hereditary chamber (see pages 43 and 72). No action had been taken then, but after the Liberal split in the mid-1880s the Conservatives' massive majority meant that occasions when the Lords opposed the will of the Commons became more common. In 1893, when the Lords threw out the Liberal Home Rule Bill, the peers were attacked as wastrels, and there was a call for their House to be 'mended or ended'. The prime minister, Gladstone, told the queen that members of his party now had a positive thirst to fight the next election on the issue of 'Peers versus People'. In fact the issue was shelved. Gladstone resigned and was soon succeeded by Conservative prime ministers – Lord Salisbury, who was determined to preserve as much as possible of the old order, and then his nephew, A.J. Balfour. Under their Conservative governments, the House of Lords tended to hibernate; but when the Liberals won a great victory in 1906 it awoke with a start.

There were now 157 Conservative MPs in the Commons facing 400 Liberals: it was one of the smallest oppositions within living memory. Nevertheless, Balfour insisted that his party 'should still control, whether in power or opposition, the destinies of this great Empire'. The result was a political stalemate between the two Houses of Parliament which unleashed a great constitutional crisis, produced two general elections, threatened the very survival of the House of Lords and finally, in 1911, led to the emasculation of the Upper House.

2 The People's Budget

> **KEY ISSUE** Why did the radical budget of 1909 produce political confrontation?

a) The House of Lords and Liberal Reforms, 1906–8

Some politicians thought that the use of the veto to negate the work of the Liberal government would be undemocratic and against the spirit of the constitution. But Conservatives had ready replies to these charges. The leader of the party, A.J. Balfour, an elegant and rather world-weary man and also something of a philosopher, was never at a loss for a reply to any proposition. He believed in the 'referendal theory', the idea that the essential function of the Upper House was to turn down measures which had never been properly put before the people for their verdict. According to this view, the veto of an important measure should lead to a general election in which the issues could be put squarely before the electorate. Hence the peers were friends not enemies of the people, and their veto was entirely in harmony with democracy. But Balfour also judged that the function of the Lords was to ensure that Britain's laws were not 'the hasty and ill-considered offspring of one passionate election'. Surely only a philosopher could contradict himself so grossly! In Balfour's mind, the veto was insurance for, and a safeguard against, the democratic verdict of the people. Lord Lansdowne, the leader of the party in the Lords and a former Viceroy of India and Foreign Secretary, chipped in with the notion that the Lords preserved the 'balance' of the constitution. Their real motives, however, were probably somewhat different. Having lost the election in 1906, Balfour was under great pressure from the hardliners in the party to oppose the Liberals by every means possible, whether fair or foul, and so the veto was a convenient weapon. As for Lansdowne, who owned estates in Ireland, he was adamant that, above all, Home Rule for Ireland should be prevented and that therefore the Lords' veto had to be preserved to forestall such a calamity.

The years 1906–8 saw regular confrontations between the Liberals and the Lords. The peers did not, of course, veto every piece of legislation put before them. They were careful to leave untouched popular measures (such as the introduction of a new trade union law in 1906 and of old age pensions in 1908), whose negation might have brought down the wrath of the people on their noble heads; but they vetoed or amended out of all recognition several key Liberal measures, including several Education Bills (all designed to remedy nonconformist grievances against the Conservative Education Act of 1902, which had given so much power to the Anglican schools), a Plural Voting Bill (which would have abolished the right of certain citizens to vote more than once), a Licensing Bill (to limit the number of public houses in any given area of the country), and no less than four land bills (designed to begin the state regulation and taxation of land). According to David Lloyd George, the President of the Board of Trade in 1907, the Upper House was not the 'watchdog of the constitution', as its supporters liked to believe, but 'Mr Balfour's poodle': it would bark for him, fetch and carry for him and bite 'anybody he sets it on to'.

Many Liberals believed that the Lords were making a mockery of democracy. But what retaliatory action could the government take? Ministers could hold an early general election, but that would be costly and might not produce a Liberal victory. And, even if it did, it might not tame the Lords. They could water down their measures in an attempt to make them acceptable to the peers. Or they could give the Lords enough rope and hope that they would be clumsy enough somehow to hang themselves. The Prime Minister, Henry Campbell-Bannerman, decided that the powers of their lordships ought to be changed: instead of having a right to veto legislation, they ought merely to be able to delay measures for two parliamentary sessions. Yet how could this be achieved, when under existing procedures the House of Lords could veto any legislation, including the removal of its veto? Political stalemate had been reached when, in 1908, Campbell-Bannerman retired and was replaced as prime minister by Herbert Asquith (only the second prime minister in Britain's history not to have a landed background). Asquith became head of a government whose legislative programme was in tatters and whose members were becoming demoralised. 'The session is spoilt,' wrote a Liberal in 1908; 'Balfour and the Lords are masters of the situation.'

The dynamic element in the government was provided by Lloyd George, who now took over from Asquith as Chancellor of the Exchequer. This was a post fraught with difficulties, for in the coming financial year the government's expenditure was likely dangerously to exceed its revenue. The menacing international position, and in particular the 'naval race' with Germany, made it impossible for Lloyd George to resist calls from the Admiralty, the Conservative Party and to some extent from the general public for extra expenditure on

Dreadnought battleships, while at the same time old-age pensions, introduced the previous year, were likely to cost several million pounds more than had initially been anticipated. As if this were not bad enough, a trade depression was reducing the usual levels of government income. The Chancellor therefore had little choice but to find another £16 million in taxation from somewhere. Here was a situation that demanded the utmost ingenuity. Fortunately the 'Welsh wizard' was seldom short of bright ideas. He devised a budget not only to raise revenue but also to by-pass the Lords' veto and thus restore Liberal fortunes.

The Lords had vetoed land and licensing bills, but surely they would never dare to veto a budget. Such a thing, while not technically impossible, would be an almost unthinkable departure from parliamentary tradition. It had not happened for centuries. Lloyd George therefore decided to 'tack' land and licensing measures on to his budget, as a means of circumventing the House of Lords. Supporters considered it a master-stroke. Opponents had different ideas.

b) The People's Budget

It took Lloyd George four and a half hours of House of Commons' time to introduce his mammoth budget in April 1909. It was, he said eye-catchingly, 'a war budget ... raising money to wage implacable warfare against poverty and squalidness'. The 'People's Budget' has certainly proved to be the most famous budget in British history. Taxes on tobacco and spirits were raised, as were stamp duties and, significantly, the cost of liquor licences. Income tax was to be raised from 1s to 1s 2d in the pound (i.e. from 5 to 5.8 per cent); death duties were also to rise; and a 'supertax' of 2.5 per cent was to be introduced on incomes over £5,000 a year. The Chancellor insisted that only the rich would be hard hit by such measures. Nevertheless, the Conservatives were aggrieved.

The Opposition complained for several reasons. First, they disliked the extra taxation, which they and their supporters would have to pay. Secondly, they disliked the fact that Lloyd George was able to balance the budget without turning to 'tariff reform', a policy of imposing import taxes on foreign goods entering Britain. Many Conservatives supported this idea because it seemed likely to boost British industry, whose products would enjoy a measure of 'protection' against foreign competition, and because it would raise revenue indirectly, on the sales of foreign goods, thus enabling government to avoid burdensome direct taxation. Tories had believed that tariff reform was a necessity, but the Chancellor had shown that this was not the case, and so his budget was especially unwelcome.

Yet the most hotly contested budget item was Lloyd George's proposal for the taxation of land. His actual measures were very modest, and he believed that the new land taxes would raise no more than

£500,000 in 1909–10. (In fact, they cost more to collect than the revenue raised.) There would, for instance, be a 20 per cent tax on the unearned increase in the value of land when it was sold, together with a 10 per cent tax on the value coming to a landowner not from his own efforts but from those of former tenants. There would also be a very small tax (0.2 per cent) on the value of undeveloped land and minerals. What caused controversy was not the precise proposals but that there should be any land taxes at all. Their lordships saw them as the thin end of the wedge: however modest in themselves, they might be increased in future years, especially since they would necessitate the valuation of every acre of land in the country. Indeed, might they not be the first step in an attack on the very principle of the private ownership of land? In the past, the peers had applied their veto to such measures; but now that they had been included within a finance bill, they would surely have no choice but to swallow the unpleasant medicine. Or would they?

It used to be thought that Lloyd George was deliberately provoking the Lords into using the veto so that the Liberal government might then restrict their powers. But this now seems extremely unlikely. It is more probable that the Chancellor wanted to circumvent the peers' veto rather than to goad them into using it. Lloyd George agreed with his Prime Minister, Asquith, that amendment or rejection by the House of Lords was out of the question: 'That way revolution lies'. But it soon became clear that the Lords might do the unthinkable. The budget only passed through the Commons with the utmost difficulty, after 70 full days' discussion and 554 divisions, and it then began to receive bitter criticisms from peers. To veto or not to veto: that was the question. Tempers were running high. One duke went so far as to wish that Lloyd George and other ministers be consigned to 'the middle of twenty couple of dog hounds'. Another peer, Lord Milner, said that the Lords should refuse the bill and 'damn the consequences'. It was at this point that Lloyd George began to see advantages in a showdown with the Lords. He wrote privately to his brother in August 1909 that he 'rejoiced at the prospect' of the rejection of his budget.

In a blisteringly critical speech at Newcastle in October 1909, Lloyd George rounded on the peers, accusing them of being social parasites.

1 Let them realise what they are doing. They are forcing revolution. But the Lords may decree a revolution which the people will direct. If they begin, issues will be raised that they little dream of, questions will be asked which are now whispered in humble voices, and answers will be
5 demanded then with authority. The question will be asked: 'Should 500 men, ordinary men, chosen accidentally from among the unemployed, override the judgment – the deliberate judgment – of millions of people who are engaged in the industry which makes the wealth of the country?" That is one question. Another will be: 'Who ordained that a

10 few should have the land of Britain as a perquisite, who made 10,000
people owners of the soil and the rest of us trespassers in the land of
our birth; who is it – who is responsible for the scheme of things
whereby one man who is engaged through life in grinding labour, to win
a bare and precarious subsistence for himself, and when at the end of
15 his days he claims at the hands of the community he served a poor pen-
sion of 8d a day, he can only get it through a revolution, while another
man who does not toil receives every hour of the day, every hour of
the night, whilst he slumbers, more than his poor neighbour receives in
a whole year of toil? Where did the table of the law come from? Whose
20 finger inscribed it?' These are questions that will be asked. The answers
are charged with peril for the order of things the Peers represent; but
they are fraught with rare and refreshing fruit for the parched lips of
the multitude who have been treading the dusty road along which the
people have marched through the dark ages ...

These sentiments were probably deeply held (even though Lloyd
George accepted an earldom in 1945); but they were nevertheless cal-
culated to inflame the situation and make the rejection of the budget
more likely.

Of the Conservative leaders, Lansdowne was for rejection. Balfour,
who was said to always see all sides of every case, was more equivocal.
Whether he was pushed from behind or whether he believed in the
merits of the case for rejection no one can be certain, and in any case,
as an expert in semantic quibbles, he would probably have regarded
such a question as too blunt to admit of a precise answer. But in the
end he, like Lansdowne, decided that the veto should be used, and
neither would reconsider when the king urged them to do so. On 30
November 1909 the Upper House rejected the budget by 350 votes to
75. The Conservatives argued that this 'hotch-potch of financial legislation' was not a normal budget, designed to balance income and
expenditure, but a deliberate and dishonest attempt to force through
Parliament measures like land valuation which the Lords had already,
in their wisdom, decided to reject. They therefore felt justified in
challenging the government to call an election and offer the budget
for the judgement of the people. *The Times* endorsed their decision,
insisting that the Lords were exercising

1 an unquestionable and indispensable right which it has not been necessary to use for a long time, thanks to the wise moderation with which
upon the whole our Constitution has been worked by statesmen of all
parties. That traditional moderation ... has been abandoned by the
5 present Government; and the House of Lords has accordingly been
compelled, either to fall back upon the use of a weapon reserved for
dire emergencies or to submit to effacement as an efficient Second
Chamber ... There is no precedent for a Government avowedly pur-
suing the policy of destroying the power of the House of Lords to reject
10 or amend any measure that a temporary majority in the Commons may

be pleased to pass, whether that measure be desired or disliked by the country. But that, and nothing else, has been the declared policy of the present Government, and the Budget is merely the culmination of a design deliberately adopted and steadily pursued.

However, Asquith was appalled. He called this use of the veto 'a breach of the Constitution and an usurpation of the rights of the Commons'. For his part, Lloyd George was jubilant. The budget had been buried – but there was the 'sure and certain hope of a glorious resurrection'. He told the National Liberal Club that 'we have got them at last.' The practical result was the dissolution of parliament.

3 The Parliament Act

> **KEY ISSUE** What events led to the passing of the Parliament Act?

a) The General Election of January 1910

A general election was called immediately. The electorate could vote not only for or against the budget but on the issue of whether the powers of the House of Lords should be curtailed. Indeed the details of the budget tended to be very much pushed into the background. The real issue was 'Peers versus People', with free trade versus protection as a sub-plot. Peers took an unprecedented role in the election, though few were as outspoken as Lord Curzon, who maintained that 'all civilization has been the work of aristocracies'. At one time this defence of the hereditary principle might have aroused little controversy; but now it was eagerly seized upon and ridiculed by the President of the Board of Trade, Winston Churchill. What great picture had ever been painted by a duke, he asked, and what had an aristocrat ever invented? The House of Lords, he insisted, was full of 'doddering peers, cute financial magnates, clever wire pullers and big brewers with bulbous noses' – in short, of 'all the enemies of progress'.

The result of the election was a narrow victory for the Liberals. They lost a hundred seats but, even so, won two more seats than the Conservatives and could count on the support of Irish Nationalist and Labour MPs for a sizable majority. The fate of the budget was now decided: at long last, a full year after it had first been introduced, it was accepted by both Commons and Lords. The peers, true to the referendal theory, now had little choice but to accept the verdict of the electorate. But the wider constitutional issue was still unsettled. Asquith had to take some action, especially as politically he was the prisoner of the Irish. The leader of the Irish Nationalists, John Redmond, insisted that he would only keep the government in office if, as a precondition for the safe passage of an Irish Home Rule Bill, it removed the Lords' veto. Yet there was no agreement among Liberal ministers over the form legislation should take. A few Liberals favoured abolishing the Upper Chamber altogether, and whereas most wished to limit the Lords to merely delaying bills – as Campbell-Bannerman had proposed – there were some who wished to see the composition of the second chamber thoroughly recast. Churchill wanted to see it made into an elective assembly; but others thought that such a momentous change might enable the Lords to challenge the authority of the Commons. Moreover, it was by no means clear that the government would be able to secure passage of its measure – whatever it turned out to be – through parliament. The king, Edward VII, had told Asquith before the election quite bluntly that he would not create enough new peers to secure a Liberal majority. After the election he reiterated his refusal: the results had been 'inconclusive' and therefore the issue should be put before the electorate a second time.

Asquith decided to press ahead, despite constitutional uncertainty, and introduce legislation. The Parliament Bill was a compromise. Its preamble insisted that the government intended to 'substitute for the House of Lords as it at present exists a Second Chamber constituted on a popular instead of hereditary basis', but noted that 'such substitution cannot be immediately brought into operation'. This was an attempt to appease ministers who wanted thorough reform. The substance of the Bill laid down that the Lords should have no power to amend or veto a money bill, that they could only delay other bills for a maximum of two years – thus, in technical language, losing an 'absolute' but retaining a 'suspensory' veto – and that no parliament should last for more than five years (as opposed to the existing seven). The last measure was a sop to those who were complaining that the removal of the Lords' veto would produce, effectively, one-chamber government and possibly almost a one-party dictatorship. As a safeguard against this, parliament was now to be subject more frequently to the democratic choice of the electorate.

The Parliament Bill produced intense debates, especially in the House of Lords itself, where there was a cacophony of conflicting voices. Diehards like the 87-year-old Lord Halsbury, whose speeches regularly contained the word 'Forsooth!', were against any change, for 'it was impossible to make an institution more practically useful for its purpose than the present House'. They argued that someone had to make a stand to stop the country going utterly to the dogs. Others wished to see an end to the automatic right of hereditary peers to sit and vote in the chamber and the introduction of elections, with peers being eligible to stand. Lansdowne wanted the admission of a non-hereditary element by the innovation of life peerages. But on 6 May 1910 the debate was stilled by news of the death of Edward VII.

His successor, George V, a 45-year-old sailor of limited intellect, was inexperienced in political issues. In deference to him, therefore,

Asquith arranged for a constitutional conference to settle the issue of House of Lords reform as amicably and uncontroversially as possible. For over six months members of the Liberals and the Conservatives took part in complex constitutional wranglings, over such issues as whether, in future, deadlock between Lords and Commons might be solved by joint sittings of the Commons and (a disputed number of) the Lords or by the use of a referendum. But in the end nothing was agreed, perhaps because Conservatives like Lansdowne preferred failure to a success that might unlock the door to Home Rule in Ireland.

b) The General Election of December 1910

Asquith returned to the idea that the monarch might create enough peers to ensure the passage of the Parliament Bill, providing the government won another general election. George V was reluctant to agree to such a controversial measure which, after all, would permanently change the character of the House of Lords. Asquith insisted that the threat alone would convince the peers to acquiesce in the removal of their veto, but no one could be sure that the king would not have to make good his threat. To compound his difficulties, George received contradictory advice from two of his secretaries. In the end he went along with Asquith's proposal, but only after the Prime Minister had insisted that 'there was a serious state of unrest among the working classes and if the King did anything to bring about the resignation of the Government it might do great harm to the Crown'. George V later described this pressure as 'the dirtiest thing ever done'. Yet had he stood out against Asquith's proposals, the crisis might well have escalated into a position where the future not only of the Lords but of the monarchy might have been in doubt. George V was wise to avoid an election on the conduct of the Crown.

The second general election of 1910, in December, was very much a re-run of the first, although now with a dose of electoral apathy that had not existed in January. One million fewer voters turned out, and a journalist called the campaign 'the most apathetic within living memory'. The country simply did not seem interested in the constitutional reform of the House of Lords. The Liberals won a third election victory in a row. But it had been a very close-run affair. Indeed Liberals and Conservatives were now tied on an equal number of seats (272), although Labour and Irish votes again gave the former a secure majority.

c) The Passage of the Parliament Act

The Parliament Bill was reintroduced to the Commons in February 1911. As many as 900 amendments were tabled by the Opposition, but its passage was a foregone conclusion. The House of Lords was the real arena for debate, perhaps for the last time in its long history. Asquith hoped that the Lords would pass the Bill without the need for the king to create new peerages and indeed without even the revelation of his promise to do so. After all, the Lords had often insisted in the past that their veto was merely designed to refer back controversial issues to the electorate. Now the electorate had voted twice in a year. Surely the peers could not expect a third election?

The Lords were galvanised into activity. They did not reject the Parliament Bill outright. Instead they amended it out of all recognition. A measure that was in some ways far more revolutionary appeared. Lansdowne masterminded a bill which would have produced a second chamber of about 350 members: 100 members would be peers who had held high office, elected by the hereditary nobility; 120 would be men elected by the MPs for particular regions; there would be 7 Lords Spiritual and 16 Law Lords; and finally the government of the day would appoint another 100 members, in proportion with party strength in the Commons. They would sit for 12 years, a third retiring every 4 years. The imminence of the withdrawal of their veto concentrated the minds of the House of Lords wonderfully, making the hereditary peers more liberal than the liberal government – though it should be recognised that, on Lansdowne's own calculations, his scheme would in 1911 have produced a Conservative majority in the Lords of about 18! Many judged that the peers were in a panic and were merely paying lip-service to ideals in which they did not sincerely believe. (This is the interpretation in the *Punch* cartoon on page 139.)

Asquith made it clear that, even if the composition of the Lords were to be reformed, he would still insist on the removal of its veto, and in July 1911 he revealed the king's promise to create a large number of new peers (dubbed 'puppet peers' by one journalist). The news produced uproar in the Commons. The Prime Minister was shouted down and the sitting had to be suspended, one observer deciding that the Conservatives 'behaved, and looked, like mad baboons'. Straightaway the Lords dropped the proposals for reform which had latterly been so dear to their hearts and debated the substantive issue: would they or would they not accept the Parliament Bill?

Opinions were divided. On one side were the 'hedgers'. They reasoned that the loss of the veto was undesirable but that nothing could be done to prevent it: better therefore to accept the Bill voluntarily, and at least preserve the power to delay measures for two years, than to see the chamber swamped by hundreds of new Liberal peers, whose numbers would ensure immediate passage not only of the Parliament Bill but of whatever other measures the government subsequently introduced. Balfour and Lansdowne were in this camp and urged Conservatives to acquiesce in what they saw as the inevitable by abstaining. Lord Curzon, who had been in favour of rejection before

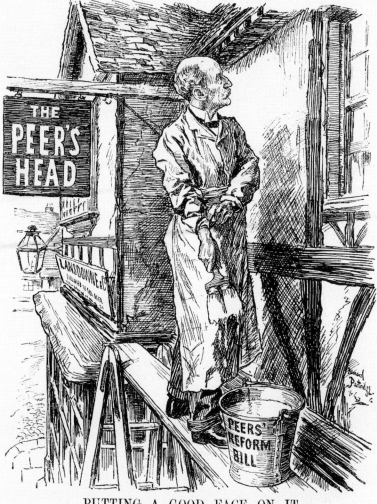

PUTTING A GOOD FACE ON IT.

LORD LANSDOWNE. "SAY THIS HOUSE IS BADLY CONDUCTED, DO THEY? AND MEAN TO STOP THE LICENCE? AH, BUT THEY HAVEN'T SEEN MY COAT OF WHITEWASH YET. THAT OUGHT TO MAKE 'EM THINK TWICE."

'Putting a Good Face on it', *Punch* cartoon, 19 April 1911.

the announcement of the king's promise, was a more vigorous champion of acceptance, convincing many peers to vote in favour of the Bill.

On the other side were the 'ditchers', those who were prepared to defy the government to the end and, metaphorically, to die in the last ditch. Many of their lordships were prepared to rebel against the guidance of Balfour, who, after all, had lost three elections in a row and had failed to provide decisive leadership. Headed by Lord Halsbury, this group contained many old-fashioned believers in the hereditary principle, often 'backwoodsmen' who had seldom attended debates at Westminster before. But this camp also contained a substantial number of politically active radical Conservatives, and their most articulate spokesmen reasoned that the Lords had nothing to lose by rejecting the Bill. Possibly Asquith was bluffing, they argued, and the king would not go through with the creation of new peers. Even if he was in earnest, George V might only create sufficient peers to allow the Parliament Bill to pass, and such a number would be inadequate for the passage of controversial legislation like a Home Rule bill. Hence the Lords would still enjoy the power of delaying measures for two years. If, on the other hand, he created 500 new Liberal lords, that would at least have the advantage of making the House so unwieldy that, sooner rather than later, fundamental reform of its composition would have to be undertaken.

The crucial two-day debate took place in the Lords on 9 and 10 August 1911. The temperature of the debate matched that of this exceptionally hot summer, 100 degrees Fahrenheit (38C) being recorded at Greenwich on the first day. No one could be confident which side would win the vote or certain of the consequences if the peers exercised their veto. Might the creation of a large number of new peers necessitate a more thorough and far-reaching reform of the Lords than that contained in the Parliament Bill, including the introduction of an elected element which could eventually claim parity with the Commons? Might the Conservatives, if they won the next election, create hundreds of their own new peers, as Lord Salisbury claimed?

As it turned out, the Lords voted by 131 votes to 114 to accept the Bill, a majority of 17. Over 300 peers had abstained, but the votes of 13 bishops and of 37 Conservative peers had given the government victory. In the end, as one historian has remarked, the upper classes had decided to go quietly, 'even though their favourite time of day was still the eleventh hour'. The Parliament Act became law later that year.

4 Conclusion

KEY ISSUE What was the significance of the Parliament Act?

a) The Origins of the Parliament Act

On one level, the Parliament Act came about because of the actions of individuals. Possibly the most important of these was Lloyd George, a representative of the new democratic ethos apparent in British politics early in the twentieth century. It has been said that he was much more inclined to blow the aristocrats a raspberry than to touch his forelock to them. However, the role of individuals has been examined earlier in this chapter. Now it is important to consider the curtailing of the powers of the Lords in terms of impersonal political trends and issues.

The clash between Lords and Commons in August 1911 represented the point at which highly charged, but distinct, political issues came together. First of all, it was the culmination of a struggle for political power between the House of Commons and the House of Lords. Of course, the Lords might possibly have voluntarily given up their veto by allowing it to fall into disuse, without its formal removal, much as the Crown had done. But, in reality, a contest had been almost certain: in a two chamber system, one assembly was bound to strive for supremacy over the other, especially when, as in 1906–11, each chamber was dominated by one of the two main parties. The struggle over the Parliament Act was thus very much a party political contest, and as such was marked by the particular concerns of Liberals and Conservatives. Victory for the Liberal government was victory for their political principles, especially Home Rule and Free Trade, as well as for Nonconformism and the temperance lobby. The Conservatives had been fighting not only to retain the power of the House of Lords but for Unionism, Protection, Anglicanism and the brewing interest.

Further dimensions to the quarrel were derived from the clash between different social groups – the landowners and the middle classes – and the two competing ideologies which they represented – traditional aristocracy and growing liberal democracy. In some ways, the Act was also a reflection of the replacement of the old agricultural order by a new industrial Britain. From this perspective, the triumph of the Commons had indeed been inevitable, given that, by 1911, agriculture was responsible for a mere 6 per cent of Britain's gross national product.

b) The Results of the Parliament Act

The Parliament Act substantially reduced the powers of the House of Lords. Never again could it affect the passage of a 'money bill' and never again could it veto any measure indefinitely. Henceforth the Lords could only reject a bill on two separate occasions: on the third time of asking (after two years), the bill would pass direct from the Commons for the royal assent. Furthermore, the Act marked an important shift of power to the Commons in the British constitution. It was no coincidence that no member of the House of Lords was ever to be British prime minister again. It was expected that the first minister should answer for the policies of his government before the elected representatives of the people.

As for the political parties, both Liberals and Conservatives were affected. The Liberals were able to introduce controversial legislation, such as the National Insurance Act, safe in the knowledge that the Lords had been tamed and could only delay measures. As for the Conservatives, they accepted the new constitutional arrangements – but they would stomach Balfour no longer. In 1911 the languid Balfour gave way to the more decisive, and certainly more middle-class, Andrew Bonar Law. The replacement of Balfour, representative of the famous Cecil family which had helped govern Britain since the sixteenth century, by a partner in an iron merchants' firm who, one peer complained, could not even recognise, let alone shoot, a pheasant, was in its way as significant an indicator of aristocratic political decline as the Parliament Act itself.

Nevertheless the Act had noticeable points of weakness. For instance, although the Lords could not affect the passage of a money bill, the definition of this term was henceforth left largely in the hands of the Speaker of the House of Commons, who ruled that not all budgets would qualify. In particular, 'tacking' was forbidden. Paradoxically, the People's Budget of 1909, whose rejection by the Lords in 1909 had started the chain of events that led to the 1911 legislation, had by this latter date been ruled virtually unconstitutional! In this respect, therefore, the Act may even be said to have increased the powers of the Lords. Certainly it prevented a more thorough attack on the Upper House and left an hereditary chamber with important constitutional powers which, on democratic grounds, have usually been considered indefensible. In particular, many have bemoaned the fact that the Act dodged the issue of reforming the composition of the Lords. Its preamble, which spoke of the intention to introduce a second chamber 'constituted on a popular instead of hereditary basis', remained a dead letter . Also, it should be noted that the conflict with the House of Lords took up a large proportion of parliamentary time in 1909–11, which might have been devoted to other measures, and, even then, did not allow the Liberals to introduce key items in their programme. Both the Irish Home Rule Bill and the Welsh Disestablishment Bill of 1912 were delayed by the Lords for two years, by which time the outbreak of the First World War made their implementation impossible.

The only other occasion on which the Parliament Act was invoked was after the Second World War, when a Labour government, after the inevitable two years' delay, further reduced the delaying powers of the Upper House, from two years to one. Clearly, therefore, the Parliament Act was used very seldom. But this was not because the Act was unimportant; it was because it helped to establish a new political atmosphere between Lords and Commons, new conventions of political behaviour, and new boundaries which the peers were unlikely to overstep. In short, the Parliament Act was an important measure, producing significant change in the name of democracy but also preserving a good deal of hereditary power. The result was a political system that was different from the pre-1911 era but also, in many respects, similar. By being willing to adapt – by 'hedging' rather than 'ditching' – the Lords had managed to survive.

Summary Diagram
The Liberals, the Lords and Reform, 1906–14

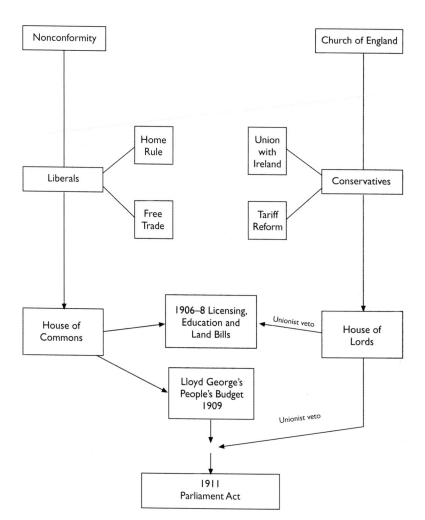

Working on Chapter 7

Making notes on this chapter should present few problems: the headings and sub-headings should help. The focus should be squarely on the Parliament Act, and you will need a detailed knowledge of the sequence of events from 1906 onwards. But do not neglect background issues like the economic decline of the aristocracy. Be sure to think critically about the relative importance of the factors involved: how important were individuals as against political philosophies?

Answering essay questions on Chapter 7

Note that a paragraph or two on the House of Lords' reform can often be fitted into general questions on the growth of democracy. But there are specific titles as well. For instance:

1. Explain why the powers of the House of Lords were reduced by the Parliament Act of 1911.

In many ways this is a 'gift' of a question. It is well worthwhile considering different ways of tackling it, and also perhaps ways in which it should definitely *not* be tackled (e.g. by a narrative of events which culminates – unless you run out of time in an exam – in the legislation of 1911). Why not sub-divide it into more manageable areas (why was there friction between the Commons and Lords after 1906? why did the Lords, in the end, accept vote for the Parliament Bill?, etc) You may well end up with 5–7 smaller questions, on each of which you could have a paragraph. You should find this technique relatively straightforward if you have practised 'structured' questions.

Source-based questions on Chapter 7

1. Lloyd George and The Times on House of Lords reform

Read the extract on pages 133 and 134, and answer the following questions:

a) Why do you think Lloyd George tied the provision of old age pensions (lines 15–17) to the issue of his budget? (2 marks)
b) Explain what was meant by 'the order of things the Peers represent' (lines 22–3). (2 marks)
c) Do you agree with The Times's judgement (line 2) that the constitution had been used with 'wise moderation' until the clash in 1909? (3 marks)
d) Use your knowledge of the period, as well as the texts, to explain which extract you find the more effective. (8 marks)

Conclusion

POINTS TO CONSIDER

Now is the time to raise your eyes from the details contained in the previous chapters and to consider the overall process of democratic reform. You need to make up your own mind about the form of democracy that has been evolved in Britain. Just how democratic is British democracy?

KEY DATES

1928 The Equal Franchise Act, giving the vote to all men and women over 21
1948 The abolition of plural voting and of the university seats; delaying powers of the Lords reduced from two years to one.
1969 Voting age reduced to 18.

Clearly the country was more democratic after the Representation of the People Act of 1918 than ever before in its history. Each of the previous reform acts – in 1832, 1867 and 1884–5 – had extended the vote and redistributed seats, so bringing democracy closer, and in 1918 a system approaching democracy had come about. A substantial majority of the adult population, comprising almost all men over the age of 21 and women over 30, could vote in general elections that had to be held at least every five years. Moreover they could vote in constituencies of approximately equal size, and provision was made to adjust constituency boundaries periodically to take account of changes in population distribution; and, after the Ballot Act of 1872 and the Corrupt and Illegal Practices Act of 1883, they could vote freely for the candidates of their choice. It was also possible for a greater variety of people than ever before to stand for parliament. No longer were there any religious restrictions on candidates – indeed prospective MPs could espouse any religion or none – and neither did they have to be especially wealthy. Every candidate had simply to pay a deposit of £150, which would be returned after the election unless he (or, for the first time, she) failed to poll one-eighth of the total votes cast. Successful candidates would then receive a salary, as they had done since 1911, thus ensuring that men and women of all social backgrounds could afford to enter parliament.

In theory Britain was governed not only by the House of Commons but by an hereditary House of Lords and the monarchy. But the monarch was really a figurehead without political power and the Lords, after the Parliament Act of 1911, could no longer reject, but could only delay, legislation. Is it not possible, therefore, to say without qualification that Britain was indeed a democracy? The answer must be no. Democracy was incomplete in 1918.

1 Further Reforms

> **KEY ISSUE** What legislation after 1918 made Britain more democratic?

The electoral system of 1918 contained clear anomalies, which prevented proper democracy. Most obvious of all was the fact that, while men could vote at 21, women had to wait until they were 30. This discrimination was devised by (an all-male) parliament to prevent women from becoming, at a stroke, the majority of the electorate, but it was unlikely to be accepted for long. In 1928 the Equal Franchise Act gave the vote to women on exactly the same terms as men. All men and women aged 21 years and over could vote, except peers, lunatics and criminals (a system that lasted until 1969, when the voting age was lowered to 18). But even this concession of universal adult suffrage did not produce a fully equal voting system: it is true that every adult could vote, but some could vote more than once. (As Orwell might have put it, all voters were equal but some were more equal than others.) The 1918 Act had merely limited, not abolished, plural voting: certain individuals could vote twice, for a constituency of residence (like everyone else) but also for one of the university seats, if they were graduates, or for a constituency in which they owned business premises. Only in 1948 was plural voting abolished, together with the university constituencies. At last a democratic system of 'one person, one vote' existed in Britain.

These reforms rectified most of the undemocratic aspects of the system that existed in 1918, though the hereditary House of Lords remained as an important part of the constitution. The Lords could delay a bill for two years, regardless of the wishes of the government or the people, and peers were regularly given ministerial offices despite the fact that they had not been elected and so represented no one but themselves. The Lords' delaying powers were reduced to one year in 1949, and life (as opposed to hereditary) peerages were introduced in 1958, but it was only after 1997 that thorough reform of the Lords began to be undertaken – with results that are still uncertain. Nevertheless, the British state was, at least in theory, close to being democratic. But was it a real democracy? Arguably the system contained (and still contains today) serious flaws.

2 Democratic Imperfections

> **KEY ISSUE** In what ways was Britain not democratic after 1918?

It was much easier to participate in politics after 1918 than it had been earlier. But, even so, economic limitations continued. Politics, like the Ritz Hotel, was open to all – but only providing they were rich enough. Election campaigns were still expensive, and if a candidate did not have the means to pay, or the support of party funds, there was little or no chance of success. In addition, the deposit of £150 was, before the effects of inflation, a substantial figure, limiting the number of independent candidates and depleting the resources of smaller and poorer parties. There can be no doubt that the choice of the electorate was limited in this way. Furthermore, the great mass of voters had no say in the choice of party candidates, who were in fact selected by small cliques in the constituency organisations from amongst a list approved by party headquarters.

General elections were no longer the rowdy, corrupt affairs seen in the early nineteenth century. But after 1918 they were dominated by the major parties, which were able to buy massive advertising and monopolise the media. Whereas the expenses incurred per candidate had been limited in 1883, no limitations had been put on the advertising and other expenses of the national party organisations. The large parties were able to raise finance from rich businessmen and sometimes from crooks (categories not necessarily mutually exclusive), who hoped to secure advantages from politicians in power; and, as a result, other candidates were at a grave disadvantage. The dominance of two or three parties has also resulted in the unwillingness of many electors to vote for minor parties or independents lest their votes be wasted and allow the party they most dislike to win. Hence many votes are cast against one party rather than positively for another.

Do British general election results really express the democratic wish of the electorate? Not necessarily. In the 'first past the post' system, the candidate who polls more votes than any other in a constituency is elected its MP. He or she may be elected by a minority of voters, and if this happened in every constituency then, in theory, a party could win every seat in the House of Commons, while polling fewer than 50 per cent of all votes. Such an extreme example has never occurred, but party strength in the House of Commons rarely reflects voting patterns in the country as a whole. For instance, in 1918, in what is generally considered the first 'democratic' election in British history since all men and most women could vote, Lloyd George's supporters won a massive majority of seats (almost 70 per cent) but only 47 per cent of total votes cast. In 1929, when there was universal adult suffrage for the first time, the Labour Party won fewer votes than the Conservatives but more seats and so went on to form a government. Since 1945 governments with workable overall majorities have invariably polled less than half the popular vote. There are admittedly advantages to this system: in particular, it makes it much easier for a party to win an overall majority in parliament and so tends to produce 'strong' government. Yet it can hardly be called properly democratic since the will of the electorate is regularly distorted.

An alternative system is 'proportional representation', whereby the number of seats a party receives is directly related to its overall total of votes. The 1918 Reform Act actually made it possible for 'PR' to be tried as an experiment in 100 constituencies, but the offer was not taken up, though recently PR has been introduced for elections to the European Parliament. Many commentators have argued that such a system has clear weaknesses: it would increase the number of parties gaining seats in the Commons, make it very difficult for any party ever to secure an overall majority and so produce a series of 'weak' coalitions. But almost everyone admits that an assembly elected by this method would reflect the wishes of the electorate far better than the present system does.

Yet if the electoral system since 1918 has been only doubtfully democratic, elections are usually the nearest Britain comes to democracy. Once a Member of Parliament is elected and a government formed, the electorate is powerless until the next election. An MP can switch from one party to another, break every promise he or she ever made, lie repeatedly to constituents and support policies which they oppose; but unless convicted of certain criminal offences, an MP cannot be removed. And as with MPs, so with governments. A government can break all its promises, introduce new policies for which it has no electoral mandate and even initiate measures which the majority of the people loathe. Ministers have sometimes seemed contemptuous of the voters, seeing them – between elections – as a nuisance to be ignored or as a group to be won over by propaganda (paid for by the electorate out of taxation). Perhaps there has existed in Britain since 1918 not so much a democracy as an 'elected dictatorship'. Voters elect a government, which then does what it wants, until the next election comes round.

One constitutional device which provides for the active participation of the people is the referendum. By this measure the entire electorate, rather than the politicians, decide key issues. In some states it is laid down that if enough electors petition for a referendum on a particular issue, then one has to be held. But this is not so in Britain, where only parliament can arrange to consult the electorate directly by this means. In British history they have done so only very seldom, distrusting this example of 'direct democracy'. Politicians have argued that such devices are not only expensive to arrange but that they are unnecessary, since the electorate elects representatives to govern not to refer issues back to the people. But critics would argue that referenda are frowned upon because they would show the yawning gap that often exists between what governments do and what the electorate wants. Certainly politicians are far less wary of soliciting the views of businessmen, lawyers, trade unionists and various 'experts'. Well-financed pressure groups often help shape policy far more than the electorate.

Is local government more democratic than central government? In practice there is little difference, except that far fewer electors bother to vote in local contests. Like the national parliament, local assemblies are dominated by party politicians, and voters have no control except in their (limited) choice at elections. Moreover, in the twentieth century the powers of locally elected bodies have declined, as central government has intervened more and more, often overriding the wishes of the local authority and the local people.

3 Verdict

> **KEY ISSUE** Is British democracy, however flawed, still valuable?

The British political system changed remarkably after 1832, so that politics became more and more representative and democratic. But the fact that change was gradual and piecemeal – evolutionary rather than revolutionary – enabled undemocratic elements from the past, like the House of Lords, to survive alongside new democratic structures. Above all, the slow pace of reform enabled the wealthy elites to accommodate themselves to democratic practices in order to retain their political power. Indeed these elites themselves fostered change in order to prevent more radical, and thorough, democratic reforms. Universal suffrage was conceded, but in stages, with the result that, although the political power of the landed aristocracy declined, the middle classes flourished. The rich in Britain, who could afford to send their sons to expensive public schools and the older universities, formed only a small proportion of the population, but they were able to dominate the House of Commons. Working-class representatives, on the other hand, were far fewer than the number of working-class voters might lead one to suppose, and the same holds true of women MPs.

Perhaps the major reason why universal suffrage did not produce a parliament which reflected British society adequately was that economic power was unevenly distributed. Everyone might have an equal vote, but candidates (and parties) who could afford to buy advertising or the services of effective agents would always be more likely to be elected than those without these advantages. Similarly, those sectors of society enjoying better education had a definite – and some might say an unfair – advantage in politics. Many political philosophers believe that a true democracy demands not just a fair electoral system but a society in which, if everyone is not actually equal, there is at least equality of opportunity for all people. Otherwise a society with impeccably democratic machinery might be no more than a sham democracy.

But can there be such a thing as a fully democratic society, outside the world of make-believe Utopias? Liberal democratic regimes exist, but they tolerate vast inequalities of wealth and power in the name of freedom. After all, what is the alternative? It might well take a dictatorship to produce the social equality which democracy requires to be truly democratic!

Democracy is therefore always imperfect, and the British example which evolved between 1832 and 1918, and which is still substantially with us today, is no exception. But despite faults and limitations, Britain is substantially a democracy. The essence of its system of representative parliamentary democracy is the right of electors – comprising almost the entire population since 1918 – to choose at a general election which of the two or three main parties should form a government. This is a limited, and some might say unsatisfactory, choice but an absolutely crucial one. Britons can get rid of their rulers, and do so peacefully – an inestimable constitutional safeguard against the unfortunate fact that all governments are composed of frail human beings and therefore are, or become, unfit to govern. As a result, Britain has been one of the most democratic countries in the world since 1918, immensely more so than the brutal despotisms of the old Soviet empire and many 'Third World' countries today. But just as the growth of democracy from 1832 to 1918 was not an inevitable process, neither is its continuance automatic. As the radicals of the nineteenth century realised, 'eternal vigilance' is needed to prevent any system becoming unresponsive to the popular will.

Working on Chapter 8

Now is your chance to grapple with the key issue of the reality or otherwise of British democracy by 1918. This will involve recognising both the strengths and weaknesses of the British system and coming to your own overall verdict. How important do you think the electoral machinery is, compared with the spirit with which that machinery is operated? Does a 'true' democracy have to operate in the best interests of the majority of the people (i.e. does it have to be government 'for', as well as 'of' and 'by', the people)? There is plenty of scope for a variety of different viewpoints. To help you make up your mind, tackle the following question: 'How democratic a country was Britain in 1918?'

Further Reading

Much has been published in recent years on issues covered in this book, and therefore students could, theoretically, undertake an unlimited amount of further reading. It is possible here to recommend only a small number of books, many of which have helpful bibliographies.

The unreformed electoral system
There are two important revisionist studies of the pre-1832 system: **Frank O'Gorman**, *Voters, Patrons and Parties: The Unreformed Electorate of Hanoverian England, 1734–1832* (Oxford University Press, 1989) and **John A. Phillips**, *The Great Reform Bill in the Boroughs: English Electoral Behaviour, 1818–1841* (OUP, 1992). Both are 'defences' of the old system and need to be read alongside more traditional accounts, for instance those provided by **Norman Gash**, *Aristocracy and People: Britain 1815–1865* (Edward Arnold, 1979) and **John Cannon**, *Parliamentary Reform, 1640–1832* (Cambridge University Press, 1980).

On radicalism and the pre-1832 reform movements, two works are fundamental: **Thomas Paine**, *Rights of Man* (1791–2, various recent editions) and **Christopher Hill's** chapter 'The Norman Yoke' in his *Puritanism and Revolution* (Mercury Books, 1962).

The Politics of Electoral reform
There are numerous detailed studies on the process of reform. Probably the best single work on the 1832 Act is **Michael Brock**, *The Great Reform Act* (Hutchinson, 1973), while the two standard works on the 1867 Act are **F.B. Smith**, *The Making of the Second Reform Bill* (Cambridge University Press, 1966) and **Maurice Cowling**, *1867: Disraeli, Gladstone and Revolution* (Cambridge University Press, 1967). Cowling sees the Second Reform Act as essentially the product of politicians manoeuvring for power; Smith gives a more balanced account. On the period between the Second and Third Reform Acts, see **H.J. Hanham's** *Elections and Party Management: Politics in the time of Disraeli and Gladstone* (Harvester Press, 1978), while the most detailed account of the 1884–5 reforms is provided by **W.A. Hayes**, *The Background and Passage of the Third Reform Act* (Garland Publishing, 1982). **Martin Pugh's** research on the Fourth Reform Act is contained in *Electoral Reform in War and Peace 1906–18* (Routledge, 1978): he has sought to correct the old interpretation that women were enfranchised almost solely because of their work in the First World War.

A most useful work covering political reformers and reforms from the late-eighteenth century to the First World War is **John Belchem**, *Popular Radicalism in Nineteenth-Century Britain* (Macmillan, 1996). The same author's *Class, Party and the Political System in Britain 1867–1914* (Historical Association, Blackwell, 1990) is a stimulating, controversial interpretation. For the Liberal party, see **G.R. Searle**, *The Liberal*

Party: Triumph and Disintegration, 1886–1929 (Macmillan, 1992); for the Tories, see **John Ramsden**, *An Appetite for Power: A History of the Conservative Party since 1830* (HarperCollins, 1999).

On the Parliament Act of 1911, see **Neil Blewett**, *The Peers, the Parties and the People: The General Election of 1910* (Macmillan, 1972). There is also useful material in general studies of the prewar Liberal governments. Useful background information is provided in **David Cannadine**, *The Decline and Fall of the British Aristocracy* (Yale University Press, 1990), which is also valuable for rural local government. On municipal government, there are numerous specialist studies. **D. Fraser** (ed), *Municipal Reform and the Industrial City* (Leicester University Press, 1982) is particularly recommended for those who wish to delve into urban reform. One of the small number of readable general accounts is **K.B. Smellie**, *A History of Local Government* (Allen and Unwin, 1968).

For women's suffrage, an excellent starting points is **Paula Bartley**, *Votes for Women 1860–1928* (Hodder & Stoughton, 1998).

On the monarchy, an indispensable – and extremely witty – source is **David Cannadine's** chapter in **E.J. Hobsbawm** and **T.O. Ranger** (eds), *The Invention of Tradition* (Cambridge University Press, 1983). There are many biographies of Queen Victoria, but perhaps the most accessible is **Dorothy Thompson**, *Queen Victoria: the woman, the monarchy and the people* (Pantheon Books, 1990). **G.H.L. Le May**, *The Victorian Constitution* (1979), has a useful section on the political role of the monarchy.

Biographies

Biographies can provide fascinating insights into politicians and their policies, but use them selectively, concentrating on the relevant sections. In a Disraeli biography, for instance, read the sections on the 1866–7 reform crisis and on his relationship with Queen Victoria. The following are particularly recommended:

John Belchem, *'Orator Hunt': Henry Hunt and English Working-Class Politics* (Oxford, 1985)

James Epstein, *The Lion of Freedom: Feargus O'Connor and the Chartist Movement, 1832–1842* (Croom Helm, 1982)

Norman Gash, *Peel* (Longman, 1976)

Eric Evans, *Sir Robert Peel: Statesmanship, Power and Party* (Routledge, 1991)

Robert Blake, *Disraeli* (Eyre & Spottiswoode, 1966)

Paul Smith, *Disraeli: a brief life* (Cambridge, 1996)

H.C.G. Matthew, *Gladstone 1809–1898* (Oxford, 1990)

Richard Shannon, *Gladstone* (2 vols., Penguin, 1999)

Andrew Roberts, *Salisbury: Victorian Titan* (Weidenfeld, 1999).

Index